BURNOUT TO ENGAGEMENT

Mindfulness in Action

ASSAAD MOUNZER, MD, MA, ACC, FACS

BALBOA.
PRESS
A DIVISION OF HAY HOUSE

2018

Balboa Press books may be ordered through booksellers or by contacting:

Balboa Press
A Division of Hay House
1663 Liberty Drive
Bloomington, IN 47403
www.balboapress.com
1 (877) 407-4847

Because of the dynamic nature of the Internet, any web addresses or
links contained in this book may have changed since publication and
may no longer be valid. The views expressed in this work are solely those
of the author and do not necessarily reflect the views of the publisher,
and the publisher hereby disclaims any responsibility for them.

The author of this book does not dispense medical advice or prescribe the use
of any technique as a form of treatment for physical, emotional, or medical
problems without the advice of a physician, either directly or indirectly. The
intent of the author is only to offer information of a general nature to help
you in your quest for emotional and spiritual well-being. In the event you use
any of the information in this book for yourself, which is your constitutional
right, the author and the publisher assume no responsibility for your actions.

Any people depicted in stock imagery provided by Thinkstock are models,
and such images are being used for illustrative purposes only.
Certain stock imagery © Thinkstock.

Print information available on the last page.

ISBN: 978-1-5043-9628-8 (sc)
ISBN: 978-1-5043-9630-1 (hc)
ISBN: 978-1-5043-9629-5 (e)

Library of Congress Control Number: 2018900884

Balboa Press rev. date: 02/16/2018

CONTENTS

ACKNOWLEDGEMENTS

I acknowledge my wife Carla for keeping up with me during all these years of happiness, friendship, camaraderie and sometimes sadness and struggles--like most lives are. I appreciate her love and gentleness, her amazing skills in raising our children and her talented cooking skills. I acknowledge my children, who are the pupils of my eyes and the most cherished people on earth for Carla and me.

My daughter, Cyma, who did the first editing of this book, is smart, talented, beautiful, gentle, and will go far in life.

My twins are Christina and Christopher. Christina, my second beautiful daughter, is dedicated, perceptive and has an amazing sense of curiosity to learn more and excel in her life.

Christopher, a wonderful man, who is full of compassion, kindness, and devotion to his growth and advancement, can do anything he wants towards being successful in this journey called life.

I would like also to thank Thomas Crowe who did a great job editing my book, I appreciate his wisdom and support.

DEDICATION

I dedicate this book to my mother, Samira Mounzer, who is an outstanding woman, dedicated, honest, perseverant, loving, and generous —just to name a few of her qualities. She instilled within my family a sense of duty and responsibility--to be the best we can be--and gave us a set of values that took us very far in life.

There is no doubt in my mind that my brother Khalil and I owe part of our success to her persistent encouragement for us to become mature, productive, kind and caring human beings.

PREFACE

"Not all of us can do great things, but we can do small things with great love"

-Mother Teresa

The reason I am writing this book is personal – very personal. It is about my journey during a tumultuous time in what used to be called the "Switzerland of the Middle East." It is about an adventure from Medical School to Residency, during a war which was devastating to my native country, Lebanon, and the life transitions that I went through, ending up in immigration and settling in a new country, learning new skills, and experiencing many challenges that enriched my life on many levels.

In this personal journey, I have included my struggles and experiences with some of the most challenging survival questions that trouble our mind while we are growing up (and we never stop growing up): What is life? What is death? What is happiness? What am I supposed to do to become important and successful? How do I get there? What if I do not make it? How do I stay healthy? How do I impress people?

And later on, more existential questions arise: Is that all that there is? What is next? What is my purpose in life? How do I fulfill my life's mission? How do I find meaning in all that has happened to me? Am I making any difference in this world?

Of course, a lot of questions remain unanswered, and the more I live and learn, the more fascinated I am with life and its complexity and sometimes its simplicity. We can make it easy and simple or we can make it painful and complex.

Looking back, I feel grateful to all the teachers, friends, family members, and total strangers, who were kind enough to guide me, love me, inspire me and show me the way.

This book includes many chapters about our struggles as human beings, professionals, and as physicians, with our anxiety, perfectionism, fear, and disappointments. It also includes tools for practicing self-care on all levels (physical, emotional, mental, and spiritual), building resilience, avoiding burnout, and finding meaning in our careers and lives. This book is for everyone who is looking to grow and find purpose in their lives.

I have included some touching stories of my patients who helped heal me while I was healing them. The names have been completely changed for privacy and confidentiality.

I've found that there are no easy answers or quick fixes to anything. This is a self-help book that you can read and keep, reminding yourself often about the importance of creating the discipline to learn a daily practice, and to be able to be genuinely happy, fulfilled, while creating sustainable results.

I also talk about spiritual psychology, coaching and mindfulness practice, and how these have transformed my life in a positive way that have made me more aware of the blocks and challenges which were interfering with my growth. I learned to move forward, to live in the present, to learn from the past, and to plan for the future without obsessing about it.

Life is short and unpredictable. It is wiser to spend it the way we choose to, remembering what is important to us and how we want to try every day to stay healthy, happy, and fulfilled.

This book is also about building new habits and learning new skills to assist you, the reader, in staying healthy, engaged, and genuinely happy. It is about your right to thrive, grow, and fulfill your mission. It is about learning the basics of self-care and mindfulness, to live a more fulfilling, and meaningful life.

Here, I have tried to offer some recommendations, shared experiences, and self-care techniques to reinvigorate your spirit. At the end of many of the chapters, I have also included some reflections, self-care techniques, and self-nurturing processes that you can use daily to help you navigate the changes affecting your life in a healthy, and proactive way.

The only requirements are an open mind and an open heart, as well as the willingness to try something different.

Listen to your inner wisdom, practice new skills diligently, and bring your most cherished values into your daily life. You have the right to treat yourself with compassion and reverence. You are the most precious person in your life, and if you do not take care of yourself, you cannot take care of others. With this dictum you will live a meaningful life in alignment with your values.

Please be sure to remember that there is no perfection in this world – you are going to fail and have to get up and try again. Practice makes it perfect. This is not a quick fix like our culture pushes us to do – this is a lifestyle change.

Mastery, as George Leonard said, requires/diligence,/commitment, and action, as well as setting your priorities, acknowledging the negative, accentuating the positive, and staying on the path.

"Fear is a natural reaction to moving closer to the truth," Pema Chodron said, in her book *When Things Fall Apart*. You are going to experience fear, doubt, anxiety, depression, and hopelessness. This is normal. So just stay on the path and keep practicing positive habits and positive thoughts, and have faith.

Thank you for reading this book, thank you for persevering, and thank you for listening (to your heart).

BURNOUT TO ENGAGEMENT

Mindfulness in Action

"A storm may be raging at the surface, but the depths remain calm. The wise man always stays connected to the depths. On the other hand, he who knows only the surface and is unaware of the depths is lost when he is buffeted by the waves of suffering."

-Matthieu Ricard

CHAPTER 1

A PERSONAL JOURNEY

"The true wisdom is in recognizing our own ignorance"

-Socrates

As a young surgeon, I was proud of what I had achieved in my life. I struggled, suffered, and was humiliated, but finally there I was, getting ready to see my first patient in private practice.

I was nervous and excited at the same time. I knew I had enough training to handle any urological problems, but I had thousands of questions and concerns. What if the patients do not like me? What if they do not understand my accent? What if they do not accept me as a foreigner to treat them or what if they do not trust me enough to confide in me?

I was starting my new practice in a small town in Southwest Virginia called Bluefield. I did not know much about the people and the culture there. I had completed my residency in Chicago, where I did not interact much with my neighbors – I was too busy with the tough residency training program.

1

"Thank you for sitting down and talking to me," were the first words one of my new patients in Bluefield told me before he left. That was a revelation to me. Wasn't I supposed to do that as a physician? I got the same feedback several times after that with other patients.

At that point, I realized that all people really wanted was someone to listen to them and give them the appropriate time they needed to feel genuine care and support from their healthcare professionals. I was happy because it started dissipating the fears that I had regarding my accent, my national origin, etc.

Slowly, I got to know the people in Bluefield. They were very warm, affectionate, cared about each other, and valued close-knit relationships. It reminded me of the small town where I came from in Lebanon called Mehaidse/Bikfaya, which was about the same size of Bluefield. It is filled with beautiful red brick homes between the pine trees around 3000 feet above sea level, like Bluefield, and people were very affectionate, hospitable, and loving.

I am a Lebanese American. My father died when I was five years old and when my brother was three. My mother had to go to work to raise us. She would later become the first female director of a bank in Lebanon. She worked hard to provide for us. We did not have much, but we had a home, food, a great education, safety, and love.

I completed Medical School at the French Faculty, St. Joseph University, in Beirut, Lebanon and then moved to the American University Hospital (AUH), also located in Beirut, in order to complete a General Surgery and Urology residency. It was during that time that the war started in Lebanon and lasted several years-- from 1975 to 1990. Thousands of people had been killed, including my best friend, Ricardo Zablith M.D., to whom I dedicated my first book of poetry *Secrets Buried in the Sand.*

I attended AUH in 1977, which was a tough adjustment from the French system I was used to. My English was not very good, even after taking several English classes at the British Council School. I felt out of place for several months and got humiliated a few times because of my French accent and my poor knowledge of English grammar. But I did not let that discourage me. I read more books and took numerous courses to be able to integrate into a challenging new culture.

After I completed my residency at AUH in 1983, I came to the United States for a research fellowship at the University of California in San Francisco, followed by a Clinical Fellowship in Urologic Oncology and Cancer surgery at Roswell Park Institute in Buffalo, New York.

C A

N Y

The situation in Lebanon was not very good at that time, so I decided to stay in the U.S. I wrote to the American Board of Urology inquiring about what I had to do to become Board certified. They told me I had to repeat three years of my Urology education. Luckily, I was able to find a Urology residency in Chicago at the University of Illinois where I completed my training in 1988 and became Board Certified in 1990.

I moved to Bluefield, Virginia in July of 1988, to get a waiver and apply for a Green Card which would allow me to work in the U.S. I was supposed to be there for only two years, but I ended up staying in Bluefield because my practice was flourishing and I loved the people there. I was excited and full of enthusiasm and I looked forward to coming into the office to see my patients and interact with them every morning. In addition to this I was extremely busy in the operating room, performing all kinds of surgeries that I was trained to do.

Blfld
W V

At the beginning, I did not take any vacation time for two entire years because I wanted to always be available to my patients and the emergency room calls. The three conditions to be successful, I was told at the time, were availability, affability, and affordability.

I was all of those – available, affable, and affordable. I loved my practice and my patients, and I treated everyone with respect and reverence. They became like family members to me. I was concerned about their problems, listened to them with care and compassion, and tried to find the best solutions to make them as comfortable as possible.

Life was good. I became a U.S. Citizen in 1994, got married to my lovely wife, Carla, and had three beautiful children, Cyma, Christopher, and Christina.

CHAPTER 2

WHEN DEATH CAN BECOME THE ENEMY

"The natural healing force within each one of us is the greatest force in getting well"

\- Hippocrates

Harold's story

I was very engaged in my practice. On top of being a perfectionist, I worked over fourteen hours a day and alienated a lot of people including some of my employees. I knew that perfection was not of this world, but I was striving for perfection in order to reach excellence.

It worked well for a while until I lost my first patient, who we will call "Harold" here. It was a couple of years after I started my practice. I had performed a radical prostatectomy on a healthy man with prostate cancer.

Everything went well during surgery and he did not even need any transfusions. In the recovery room, and as soon as he woke up, he had a massive heart attack and died instantly.

I did not know what to do. I was devastated and did not have anyone to talk to. I went to my room and cried. I could not sleep for several nights, constantly thinking about if I could have done something different to prevent his death. Of course, there was no answer.

After that, I took nothing for granted. I knew that life was not black and white, but rather a large grey area where everyone is different, where our needs are different, and each person's perspective is different.

Later on, his son told me that Harold knew he was going to die and that he had previously shared that with his family. I was shocked; if I knew that, I would not have operated on him. Sometimes, patients have a sixth sense of what is going to happen to them and we need to respect that and explore it with them. We need to trust that their inner healing mechanism is at work and needs to be in the picture for every decision they make.

At this point in my career I started focusing on the life of my patients more than on my surgical skills. I was carefully evaluating every one of them and talking to them in detail about their fears and their expectations so that I could understand them better.

Gradually, I started suffering from empathy fatigue. I started worrying about every one of my patients in the same way that I worry about members of my family. I was bringing home their pain and suffering, their problems, their pathology, and even started experiencing emotional exhaustion and burnout. I was feeling physically and emotionally exhausted at the end of each day, was not sleeping well, became irritable, and sometimes irrational.

I knew I needed to do something. "What is next?" "What am I supposed to do now?" were the questions that haunted me for a long time!

A few years earlier in Chicago I had learned about a training program called "Insight" that was affiliated with the University of Santa Monica and which offered a Master's degree in spiritual psychology. Earlier, I had tremendously enjoyed the Insight training in Chicago that had opened my heart in such a wonderful way. In that environment I had felt safe expressing my deepest feelings of insecurity and fear in a loving, supportive group. I remembered learning new skills, making new friends, and becoming less anxious and more centered.

So, I decided to enroll in the psychology program. I had to travel to Santa Monica one weekend per month for two years to complete the training that included out-of-class readings, homework, and papers to write. It was one of the most wonderful things I ever did for myself. I learned new skills to help care for myself. I learned about self-forgiveness and personal responsibility, about reframing beliefs, and using challenges and difficulties as stepping stones for my inner growth. I had never learned these skills in medical school and, in fact, had not even heard of personal growth at that time.

In school, our lives, as physicians, were about studying, learning technical skills, performing procedures, taking care of our patients, and having to be perfectionists with no room for mistakes. I did not even know what the concept of self-care or self-forgiveness meant.

In the psychology course I found a master teacher within myself called "Inner Counselor" or "Authentic Self" which helped me to find the answers I sought within myself. I started taking better care of myself and learned that self-care happens at many levels: physical, mental, emotional, and spiritual. This was a foreign concept in medicine at the time because we were taught to only take care of people on a physical level.

I found that I started listening to my patients better, relating to their problems, understanding them, and, at the same time, keeping their problems away from my personal life. I was feeling compassion for them and desired to relieve their suffering without their problems interfering with my own sanity and my own health. I started a prostate cancer support group which was very successful. This group was based upon the idea that men, in general, do not like to share their feelings. I came to find out that it was the first Prostate Cancer support group in Southwest Virginia and Southern West Virginia.

I started facilitating stress management workshops for physicians and nurses because I understood how much pressure they were experiencing and how it was affecting them in a negative way. It also helped me control my own stress-related issues and to learn several additional coping mechanisms.

CHAPTER 3

STRESS AND BURNOUT

"Health is a state of complete physical, mental, and social well-being and not merely the absence of disease or infirmity"

-World Health Organization

My history with burnout is a recurring theme. Sometimes we think we have conquered the beast, but in fact, stress has crept up on us in a very subtle way. New regulations, liability issues, and emergency calls are only a few of the factors that physicians face every day.

Burnout happened again when our twins were born. We were elated to have twins, and at the same time we were exhausted –- waking up at night, caring for three kids, and working full time. I hated it when I was called at night and I resented every call from the emergency room. I felt as though they were invading my private life, my sanity, and my right to be happy.

All of this eventually led to depression (probably projected as sympathy for my wife). It was almost funny because I had never heard of "postpartum depression for dads" before that.

Unfortunately, as human beings we fall back into our old habits very easily and somehow forget about all the tools for self-care that we previously learned and knew were important for us. It parallels all the New Year's resolutions that most of us make every year about going on a healthy diet or starting an exercise program and only a few of us keeping the discipline for long enough to create new habits.

So, what is" burnout?" Burnout is a state of distress and inefficient coping with chronic stress. It is a syndrome that harbors multiple symptoms, including depersonalization (with the customer or the patient becoming an object), emotional and physical exhaustion, a sense of low personal accomplishment, and loss of meaning at work.

Burnout leads to decreased effectiveness and loss of enthusiasm. Eventually, burnout can lead to depression, alcohol and drug abuse, and suicidal ideation. Burnout can affect people of all ages--men, women, and even children sometimes. It does not only affect the physical body, but also emotional and mental health.

To understand burnout, we need to understand the physiology of stress and the "fight or flight response" (described by Walter Cannon in 1932). Now, "the freeze response" has been added in cases of patient helplessness. Stress can be the result of external stressors or internal like the perception of a physical or psychological threat. It is an imbalance between demands and resources (the ability to cope). Different people react to stress in different ways. The way we perceive the threat of stress is what creates the chemical and physiological reactions within us which affect our mind, body, and emotions.

Eustress (as described by Hans Selye) is positive stress when it is constructive, short lived, and pleasant. In these situations, the "fight or flight" response is often associated with increased performance and success in today's business environment. For example, before an athletic event, competitors involuntarily elicit this response.

Before an examination, some students exhibit increased heart rate and blood pressure, their adrenaline is pumping and Dopamine is increasing, therefore improving their performance.

"Flow" is the ultimate eustress experience. It is exemplified by being focused on a challenge, fully present, absorbed, and exhilarated. Dopamine creates in us the sensation of pleasure and is our primary reward system. Endorphins also secreted during Eustress maximize our capacity to achieve the reward. This is our "success system." Endorphins increase our motivation, increase our confidence, decrease pain, and reduce depression and anxiety.

On the other hand, Distress is negative stress when it may lead to anxiety, irritability, exhaustion, withdrawal, and depressive behavior. It happens when stress is repeated without rest or when the perception that one's response is inadequate to cope with a physical or psychological threat. Some of these so-called "threats" are real and include major life events, trauma, accidents, natural disasters, physical and emotional abuse, terrorist attacks, environmental stress, and death.

Other sources of stress for employees could be conflicts in company, lack of job security, the way employees are treated by their bosses, unclear expectations, poor communication, inadequate pay or benefits, long work hours, or relationship conflicts. Surprisingly, the stress response is also elicited when our beliefs have been challenged, whether religious or political. Dr. Jonas Kaplan, a psychologist from the University of Southern California, describes in his research (published in the journal "Scientific Reports") that when our deeply-held beliefs are challenged, we would react as we would to other threats. He showed that the *amygdala* and the *insula*, the regions of the brain related to stress and anxiety, light up (on an MRI), and people become hard-headed and defensive rather than calmly listening and considering the evidence.

11

"Stress" is the term used to define the body's automatic physiologic response to the demands placed on our body and mind.

When we are faced with such events, believing that our mechanisms of defense are ineffective, we start suffering from the negative results of stress. Our mind triggers a series of biochemical reactions to get our body ready to deal with stress. There is central activation of our nervous system, alertness, cognition, vigilance, and focused attention. This is due to the production of Epinephrine, Corticotropin, Cortisol, Oxytocin, Dopamine, and Endorphins.

The central activation is followed by peripheral activation: increased metabolism, increased blood pressure and heart rate, increased breathing, increased muscle tone, and blood flow to large muscle groups.

Containment or "adaptive coping" (eustress) occurs to prevent burnout. It involves auto-regulation, in which the increase of Cortisol inhibits the secretion of ACTH from the hypothalamus by a feedback mechanism. Thus, inhibiting further activation of the HPA (Hypothalamic-Pituitary-Adrenal) axis. The ability to create Eustress (stress management techniques, mindfulness, and relaxation) is necessary for achievement, sensation of well-being, and positive attitudes, thus increasing work performance.

Dysregulation (distress) can occur in one of four ways: repeated stress without rest, lack of adaptation to a repeated stress, inadequate activation of the stress response, or inability to shut off the stress response.

The "fight or flight" response was a mechanism that our ancient ancestors who lived in the wilderness used in order to protect themselves. On the other hand, the fight or flight response is also elicited frequently in a person who cannot fight or run. For example, if you are stuck in a traffic jam during rush hour every day for a long period of time, you can continually experience high blood pressure, heart disease, anxiety, migraines, digestive disorders, chronic fatigue, sleep problems, weight gain, and chronic pain.

Other stress warning signs could include irritability, restlessness, tiredness, compulsive eating, excess smoking, loneliness, trouble thinking clearly, lack of creativity, constant worry, forgetfulness, loss of sense of humor, emptiness, loss of meaning, intolerance, resentment, and lack of intimacy. Chronic stress can also lead to depression, cancer, and impairment in memory and concentration (E-newsletter, Mayo clinic, Oct 2016).

Current research from the University of Montreal, published in February 2017, has shown that prolonged exposure to work-related stress for over twenty years has been linked to an increase likelihood of lung, colorectal, and stomach cancer, as well as non-Hodgkin lymphoma. In their study, the most stressful jobs included firefighters, industrial engineers, aerospace engineers, mechanic foremen, and vehicle and railway-equipment repair workers.

Physicians have their own stressors. They are bombarded with stressful events including a very sick population, family issues, excessive workload, inadequate support, loss of autonomy, lack of self-care, and threat of litigation and malpractice suits, which make their lives very challenging with unrealistic expectations.

A study was done on the stress levels in General Practitioners (GPs) and hospital consultants by Caplan[1] in 1994 showing that 47% of workers scored high on their questionnaire for high levels of stress. 27% of the GP scores showed they were very depressed, and 54% of workers suffered from anxiety while being at the hospital.

These statistics are extremely alarming! Studies by Tait Shanafelt[2], MD, the Director of the Physician Well-being Program at Mayo clinic, demonstrated that 45.8% of physicians reported at least one symptom of burnout compared to 33% of the regular U.S. population in 2012. This incidence has increased to 55% in 2015 according to follow-up research by the same author[3] in a survey of 15,800 physicians in over 25 specialties. Critical Care, Emergency Medicine, and Urology were on top with an incidence of 55%, with Family medicine and Internal medicine at 54%, Pediatrics at 53%, Surgery, OB/GYN, and Neurology at 51%, and Cardiology, Radiology, and Anesthesiology at 50%.

Female physicians had a higher incidence of burnout than male physicians did. 7% of physicians contemplate suicide every year and many actually do commit suicide--with 400 doctors committing suicide in 2015, which is double the national average. Although more women try to commit suicide than men, more men actually die from their attempts because a lot of them use firearms while women almost always use pills. A study published in the Archives of Surgery in 2012[4] showed that the prevalence of alcohol abuse and male surgeons' dependence on it was 13.9%, while for female surgeons it was 25.6%.

On top of that, physicians who are experiencing burnout commit more mistakes, often have errors in judgment, and may cause patients harm.

Residents in training, as well as medical students, also have a high rate of depression, burnout, and suicide. It is easy to imagine how critical this is. Many doctors who die from suicide are sometimes outwardly and seemingly the kindest and most well-adjusted people. "Doctors are masters of disguise. Even fun-loving, happy docs who crack jokes and make patients smile all day may be suffering in silence," Dr. Pamela Wible shares in her fascinating book *Physician Suicide Letters.*

Many techniques have been developed to deal with the consequences of stress and considerable research has been conducted on the prevention of stress. A number of self-help approaches to stress-prevention and resilience-building[5] have been developed, including cognitive behavioral therapy and mindfulness.

As for my personal journey, it took several months before the road to sanity started appearing again. I had lost the discipline of self-care and felt the need for another "booster shot." In 1997, I went for a third year of psychology training and learned about "universal consciousness" and receiving guidance from beyond. In this sense, it was all about starting to trust my intuition and the importance of spiritual guidance.

Reflection

By exploring answers to the following questions about yourself and your reactions to challenging life events, you may discover how you can respond effectively to difficult situations.

Get a journal and begin by answering the following questions as suggested by the American Psychological Association:

- *What kinds of events have been most stressful for me?*
- *How have those events typically affected me?*
- *Have I found it helpful to reach out to important people in my life when I am distressed?*
- *What have I learned about myself and my interactions with others during difficult times?*
- *Has it been helpful for me to assist someone else going through a similar experience?*
- *Have I been able to overcome obstacles, and if so, how?*
  - *What has helped make me feel more hopeful about the future?*

CHAPTER 4

SELF CARE

"Each patient carries his own Doctor inside him. We are at our best when we give the doctor who resides within each patient a chance to go to work."

-Dr.Norman Cousins

It seems to me that I have gone through many "midlife crises" in my life. I like to call them "awakenings," because in retrospect every one of them was a new chapter and a new learning and growing experience. Every time I attended a personal growth training event, I felt renewed, rejuvenated, and learned so many skills to help me live a happier life.

Reviewing some of the projects we had at the University of Santa Monica, a specific one that caught my eye was called "Self-Mastery through Self-Management." They taught us to decide what qualities we needed to complete the project and to form an affirmation around that. We had weekly strategies for success that were implemented every week to achieve our goals. We had to write down what we did every day and keep our goals SMART (Specific, Measurable, Achievable, Realistic, and Timely). It was self-care on all levels: physical, emotional, mental, and spiritual.   SMART

I meditated three times a week, exercised twice a week, ate healthy, and reframed my beliefs about myself. I released all my self-doubt and replaced it with enthusiasm. In addition to self-care, we were instructed to design a project and follow it to successful completion.

My project was to create a workshop for healthcare professionals, introducing the concept of healing, and explaining the humanistic approach to medicine. In 1993, this was considered a bold workshop to present to physicians since they were anchored in the scientific approach to medicine. At least outwardly, the idea of applying any spiritual connection to our work was being dismissed. I was a little scared and very skeptical about the completion of that project.

The qualities I chose that were needed to be able to complete the project were enthusiasm, courage, and self-confidence. In this, we learned to write affirmations and mission statements to support us in our endeavor. My own affirmation was, "I am confidently and enthusiastically achieving my goals, courageously expressing myself, and enjoying success, happiness, and freedom."

I worked diligently for several months to create the outline of the workshop: how many parts it would be, who the ideal audience would be, specific goals, short term and long term goals, how to achieve them, and arranging for a pilot presentation. I did a lot of readings by masters in the field – Bernie Siegel, Rachel Naomi Remen, Deepak Chopra, Wayne Dyer and even attended workshops with some of them. I took voice lessons and speech dynamic lessons to improve my presentation skills--all with the support of a dynamic group of students to provide feedback and positive reinforcement. All during this process, I depended on a higher power to guide my steps.

Finally, there was success. In June 1993, I addressed a group of physicians on the subject of "The Wisdom of Healing"--explaining the new-model-medicine and how we need to look at every patient as a whole, not only as a case or a disease. I emphasized the importance of caring, compassion, heart centered listening and how we can improve patient communication.

I was shaking when I began the lecture, but after a while I became comfortable and was surprised by the positive feedback of the participants at the end of the presentation. For me, it was a milestone in my new career as a speaker and an advocate for healing.

Since then, I have facilitated many workshops for physicians and nurses about health and healing. I also worked with the public to explain the concept of self-care and how it can positively influence our immune system. I facilitated cancer support groups and worked in association with the American Cancer Society and hospice to create the "We Can Cope" program that was presented to cancer patients and their families.

Throughout this challenging time, having a positive and optimistic attitude while nurturing myself and my "inner child" were keys for successful completion. Having the support of my group and team members was especially important to stay motivated and to move forward.

Fear and self-doubt were also part of the process. I learned that processing through the fear while continuing my "action steps" was a great way to succeed. I learned that supporting myself unconditionally, using self-forgiveness and admitting that I am not perfect were valuable keys for success, as well.

In 2003, I was overwhelmed again by the pressure of a busy stressful practice and I found that I was losing my center again.

Assaad Mounzer, MD, MA, ACC, FACS

There were more and more regulations being created and affecting our practice: more paperwork, computer work, and restrictions from the government or big corporations. We could not take vacation time if we could not find someone to cover for us; the needs of the patients were greater; and there were not enough physicians to cover for everything.

Liability insurance was now very high and the cost of medical care skyrocketed because of all the unnecessary tests that physicians were ordering to protect themselves from a malpractice suit. Administrators, lawyers and nurses were taking control of all the administrative and political aspects of medicine because physicians were busy taking care of their patients.

In my personal life, I was becoming irritable and impatient. Once, I screamed at my daughter because she was not listening to what her mother was saying. Of course I felt bad afterwards, not wanting my children to hate me. It was already enough that I had missed half of their basketball games or ballet recitals just because I had to work late. It seemed I was always on call? The demands were never-ending.

With my stress meter rising daily, I signed up again for a new program in Spiritual Psychology called: "Emphasis on Consciousness, Health, and Healing" at the same university where I'd gotten my earlier training.

During this final year, we had a project about our own health and performed weekly strategies to become healthier and happier. I remember I slowly stopped needing to take my arthritis medication and at the end of the year I was completely off the medication and the arthritic pain was gone. This was proof to me of the power of our own mind and spirit to become healthier and happier without needing to rely only on medications. It would be an understatement to say that this was another cornerstone in my personal growth and

20

the way I began to look at things from a different perspective. It taught me that we should trust the power within us to heal ourselves, and reminded me again about the concept of "inner knowing." I learned during this time to check in with my inner child when I was tired or angry and see what was bothering "him." Every time I did check in I found that it was about not having enough fun. He (I) needed more rest and relaxation.

During this time I got in touch again with the wise being called my "Inner Counselor" or my "Authentic Self," where all the answers reside. I learned to trust this, as a gift from God, and received the information with joy and gratitude. I learned to set an intention at bedtime before I went to sleep in order to receive messages from the divine – for healing, self-renewal, and clarity about next steps. I cultivated clarity of thinking and was fully aware of God's healing power as an answer to my inner work.

The key phrase or mantra for all of that was:

"I am a Soul having a human experience, and God is my partner."

Then, in 2004, I quit my successful, private practice of fifteen years because I could not take the pressure anymore. I sold my practice, took a sabbatical for a year, and started traveling. I knew I had to take care of myself first so that I could take care of others. I registered for "The Healer's Art" program at Commonweal by Rachel Naomi Remen, MD. It was a wonderful program that gave me the tools to work with medical students and residents in order to explore the awe and mystery in medicine, as well as support them in understanding and expressing grief in a loving, compassionate environment.

It was not until recently, from 2015 to 2017, that I facilitated the Healer's Art Workshop for the residents at the hospital where I live.

I'm a spiritual being, having a ⭐ earthly experience

It was such a positive experience for them – their comments and reflections about the program will be shared later in this book.

I was also interested in peace building. In 2004 I had gone to Eastern Mennonite University in Harrisonburg, Virginia and obtained certificates for peace building and conflict resolution during a summer program. Through this, I was hoping to bring some peace to my native country, Lebanon, which had been devastated by the war there.

We moved to Lebanon in August of 2004, allowing the kids to spend time with their grandparents and to learn Arabic and French in addition to their English.The experience was very enriching. I worked part time and was able to facilitate a "Health and Healing Program" at the Middle East Institute for Health where I worked. I taught cancer patients about the Mind-Body connection and the power of our mind to affect our immune system. Patients loved the program and came week after week to learn more.

In my free time, I walked the trails in the mountains of Lebanon and wrote poetry. (*Secrets Buried in the Sand,* 2016. Balboa Press). Unfortunately, the political situation was still very volatile. The prime minister was killed in February of 2005 and there were almost monthly car bombings, killing politicians and innocent people. It was unsafe to continue living there. And so, in 2006 my family and I came back to the U.S.

Now, back in the U.S. I worked as an employee for the hospital, because I did not want to deal with the administrative part of my private practice. I was happy at first with this decision, then slowly I started experiencing the same burnout symptoms again: being physically and emotionally exhausted and losing the passion and enthusiasm for my work. I was an employee, so I did not have the power to make many changes in the system which was becoming

22

increasingly restrictive and controlling. The burden of electronic medical records, increased patients volume, and lack of support was pushing many physicians to retire early or even look for a part time or administrative job.

I was dragging my feet every morning to wake up and go to a job which was not a source of passion for me as it had been when I had first started my practice. I felt that physicians were losing their grip on being in control of how medicine is practiced. It wasn't until years later that they started entering the political process in order to influence regulations and legislation and to start lobbying in order to protect their rights. But even this eventuality was "too little too late."

I was becoming restless and wanted to do something to help myself and help others. The statistics were very alarming about the rate of burnout among physicians and the increased rate of suicide. I was thinking that it was time for physicians to reclaim the humanistic part of medicine where they are the ones deciding what is best for their patients, how much time to spend with them, and how to define the quality of care. It was time for them to also learn how to care for themselves, stay healthy, and stay engaged. I wrote the *Physicians Bill of Rights* (see copy at the end of this book.). I enrolled in a coaching program to help me determine what my next step was going to be. My plan was to retire as soon as possible and start a new career of helping physicians and healthcare professionals better deal with burnout.

p99

There is no doubt that self-care is the first step to staying healthy, managing stress in an effective way, and preventing burnout. Self-care has to do with well- being, happiness, and building a good strategy at all levels: physical, emotional, mental, and spiritual. This also allows providers – once they learn how to care for themselves – to teach their patients how to do that, as well. The same process applies for every profession where workers are experiencing chronic stress and burnout.

"An ounce of prevention is worth a pound of cure."

Health is a balance between all the levels of our being: the physical, emotional, mental, social, and spiritual. An imbalance in any of these levels can create disease (Dis-Ease) and discomfort in one or more of the other levels. This may seem like a challenging task to achieve, but creating this kind of comprehensive balance is an essential way to stay healthy in mind, body, and spirit.

Sometimes, we cannot figure out why the physical body is suffering from disease, and so we have to explore an emotional or mental imbalance to be able to cure the physical ills. If someone has been abused as a child, they can suffer indirect consequences in their body without realizing it is related to the abuse. They can experience bouts of anger, depression, chronic pain, and anxiety, for example. They are needing to heal the memories of neglect, abuse, and frustration before they can move forward into becoming healthy and balanced physically. Sometimes, a physical disease is a manifestation of our subconscious screaming for help. And because we are always in a hurry; we do not give ourselves permission to grieve, celebrate, relax, play, and recuperate.

How do we become healthy and balanced? These are some ways *(5)* listed very simply.

I (On the physical level:)

 Respect your body (the temple of your soul).

Exercise daily. Even walking is important. Connect with nature. Pick a Martial Art: Yoga, Tai Chi, Karate, and Qigong. Take time

24

Fresh squeezed

for yourself. Eat Healthy. A diet made of 80% fresh vegetables and juice, whole grains, seeds, nuts, and fruits helps strengthen your immune system.

Green tea has cancer-fighting properties; it is a very strong antioxidant. Other antioxidants like Vitamin E and C are important, as well, which are found in fruits and vegetables. They protect the cells from damage believed to be linked to cancer. Some of the most antioxidant-rich foods are blueberries, red grapes, pomegranate, apricots, spinach, and essentially all red fruits. Tomatoes are rich in Lycopene and are known to fight Prostate Cancer. Omega 3 Fatty Acids, found in Salmon and other sea foods, are known to fight cancer and are good for your heart too. Nuts, especially walnuts and almonds, are rich in Vitamin E and unsaturated fatty acids.

On the emotional level:

Free your heart from hatred. Express and release your anger without hurting yourself or those around you, Anger management classes are quite helpful. Forgive yourself – this is the best medicine. Forgive others who have hurt you. Forgiveness is the key to freedom. Get coaching or counseling. Share your deepest feelings. Heal old traumatic memories. *P 99*

On the social level:

Get family support. Renew your caring relationships. Talk to a good friend. Join a support group. Watch funny movies – laughter improves your immune system. Norman Cousins, who suffered from ankylosing spondylitis, a very painful disease requiring pain medication at one point in his life, described how he stayed pain-free without meds simply by watching funny movies.

Share your experience. Stay with happy people.

On the mental level:

Modify your thoughts to positive ones. "As a man thinketh, in his heart he becomes." Win in your imagination. Practice positive affirmations. Create life goals and make them SMART (Specific, Measurable, Achievable, Realistic, and Time specific). Be careful what you wish for, you just may get it. Read inspiring books. Use visualization. Apply the relaxation response. Live in the present and be Mindful. Use Mindfulness Meditation Practice and Mindfulness Based Stress Reduction. Mindfulness practice is an essential part in this process of self-growth for building resilience and preventing burnout. It not only creates the discipline you need, but also creates the commitment needed to pursue your dreams and live a meaningful life. Life that aligns with your values in a calm and focused way.

On the spiritual level:

Take time to relax. Appreciate yourself. Love unconditionally and feed your spiritual self. Have faith. There is a reason for everything. Faith is an attitude of commitment that tends to shape our life. Research by Harold Koenig at Duke University has shown that people who have faith and practice their religion have less admissions into hospitals or emergency rooms and are generally healthier people.

Pray – prayer produces miracles. Believe in a Higher Power. Meditate. Do spiritual exercises and attend healing services. Be optimistic about the future and be of service. It is about surrounding yourself with the people you love and appreciate, and those who love you and appreciate you in return. It is about creating a support group – a spiritual family – and good habits to find your mission and meaning in life.

Practice Mindfulness. In my experience, mindfulness has helped me stay focused, pay attention to my values, set an intention for everyday, use my wisdom to learn from my mistakes, and not judge

26

my unskillful actions. It has also taught me to keep an open heart, practice loving kindness with myself and others, and use compassion to support people in relieving their suffering with equanimity and empathetic joy.

 P 100

"Service above self" is the motto we use in Rotary. This has been a great rewarding experience for me, to focus on others, every now and then, instead of focusing only on my own needs. There is so much hunger in the world for empathy and compassion. It reminds me of what Alan Wallace said, "Genuine happiness does not come from the world, rather it comes from what we bring to it."

Reflection

Take time to ponder on these reflections before you go on:

--Take the time and start a journal for your well-being and self-care.

--Divide the page in four paragraphs: physical, emotional, mental, and spiritual (see the form at the end of this book).

--Write only one thing to accomplish in each paragraph from each level.

--Practice the steps for your goal daily for two whole weeks. The third week you can add one more goal in each paragraph and practice daily for two more weeks.

--Continue the process with different goals, shifting or adding goals at your convenience. Be sure to make these goals SMART, as we said before, and in alignment with your values. This is a journey – make sure you enjoy it.

p 115

CHAPTER 5

RESILIENCE

"Remember that life is not measured by the number of breaths we take, but by the moments that take our breath away"

-Vicki Corona

There are many ways to measure stress levels and practice techniques for stress prevention and management. Psychologists can use different methods from counseling, behavioral therapy, cognitive therapy, anger management, relaxation techniques, guided imagery as a mind-body intervention, conflict resolution, etc. You can spend more time with nature, learn meditation and mindfulness, use music therapy, humor, physical exercise, time management, planning and decision making, and coaching, just to name a few.

One of the essential ways to prevent burnout is by building resilience. If you want to thrive and flourish, you are the one who needs to learn how to care for yourself and find meaning in your work. It is not something taught at schools, colleges, at home, or even in medical school. It is something that life imposes on us to learn—to learn coping skills to manage stress in a more effective way. It is something most of us cannot do alone. We need to ask for assistance, a guide,

Assaad Mounzer, MD, MA, ACC, FACS

a thinking partner, a coach, and a support group to walk with us in this journey. Self-Care is something we can learn, and skills we can nurture and practice to live a meaningful and happier life.

You are responsible for you own happiness and well-being. It is one of your inalienable rights. (Refer to *Physicians Bill of Rights* at the end of this book.)

Hospitals and big healthcare corporations are not aware of the pressure they put on physicians and the consequences to their work. Most of them do not know how to support the well-being of the physicians, and they need our guidance to create programs and workshops to keep providers happy, engaged, and to feel supported and appreciated. Most medical institutions do not realize that their number one customer is the physician – not only the patient. If there are no physicians, there is no healthcare system.

How is resilience defined? Epstein and Krasner[6], two physicians at the University of Rochester, describe resilience as "the ability of an individual to respond to stress in a healthy and adaptive way such that personal goals are achieved at minimal psychological and physical cost; resilient individuals not only bounce back rapidly after challenges but also grow stronger in the process."

It is like going to the gym. There you build your muscles, stamina, and endurance, so when you are faced with a challenging physical situation you are prepared. The same goes for resilience. With mindfulness, you train your mind to be aware, you learn to be present with your emotions, and you learn acceptance, so when a stressful situation arises, you elicit the Relaxation Response instead of the Fight or Flight response.

Being resilient does not mean that a person doesn't experience difficulty or stress. In fact, the road to resilience is likely to involve

30

considerable amounts of emotional stress while at the same time learning to cope through behavioral changes and developing daily, healthy habits. Amit Sood, M.D., in his book *Handbook for Happiness*, describes resilience as having (four) domains; physical, cognitive, emotional, and spiritual. Physical resilience is the ability to recover quickly from illness or injury. It is about having an active lifestyle, healthy eating, adequate sleep, nurturing relationships, optimal self-care, timely medical and preventive care, and a good handle on stress.

Cognitive/mental resilience is to maintain focus in the midst of stress. Attention training (mindfulness) enhances cognitive resilience.

Emotional resilience is experiencing positive emotions and quickly recovering from negative emotions. It is the ability to deal with adversity, and make the best of your limitations, by approaching rather than withdrawing from challenges.

Spiritual resilience is the ability to maintain a higher meaning and selfless perspective, despite facing adversity and disappointments.

According to the American Psychological Association, the primary factor in resilience is having caring and supportive relationships within and outside the family. Several additional factors are associated with resilience including the capacity to make realistic plans and take steps to carry them out, a positive view of yourself and confidence in your strengths and abilities, the capacity to manage strong feelings and impulses (emotional intelligence), the willingness to accept the idea that change is part of living, and to have the discipline to create a daily practice for self-discovery and personal growth.

Think of resilience as taking a raft trip down a river. You may encounter obstacles, rapids, and turns, but the changes you experience affect you differently along the way. It takes planning, perseverance, and alertness to continue the trip successfully. It takes support of trusted companions who can be helpful in dealing with upstream currents and other difficult stretches of the river.

Additional techniques to prevent burnout are to change your lifestyle, eat a balanced diet rich with minerals and antioxidants, and to spend time alone, in nature, and with loved ones.

Another ingredient in achieving resilience is to get plenty of sleep. Sleep deprivation is detrimental to your immune system. During the early slow-wave-sleep stage, a decrease in blood levels of Cortisol, Epinephrine, and Norepinephrine induce increased blood levels of the hormones leptin, pituitary growth hormone, and prolactin and the cytokine interleukin is released, which stimulates immune function.

Again, not only physicians are affected, but over 33% of U.S. workers experience burnout. There are numerous external factors causing burnout such as excessive regulation, lack of control, lack of appreciation, and lack of a support system, which, in fact, should be addressed also by big corporations and institutions. The internal factors causing burnout are lack of self-care, a perfectionist attitude, competitiveness, and the perception that one's response is inadequate to deal with stress.

We can enhance resilience by encouraging institutions and companies to start a well-being program for employees, stressing that the most important factor in healing is to learn how to care for ourselves with compassion and love.

This is a complex process and may take a lifetime of new practices and proactive actions to build a new life meaningful to yourself and the people you love.

Remember: Caring for self w/ compassion & Love

P99

1. Care for yourself enough to make your own health a top priority.
2. Live mindfully in alignment with your values. P98
3. Demonstrate gratitude and have a positive outlook on life. P100
4. Exercise on a regular basis.
5. Take time to regularly rest and connect with nature.
6. Adapt to change and suffering – build resilience.
7. Use acceptance and equanimity. Acceptance is the foundation for developing inner peace, stability, strength, and wisdom.
8. Invest in meaningful relationships.
9. Forgive yourself and others repetitively. P99
10. Have a purpose and higher meaning for your life. Be of service. P100

We need to stop here for a moment and see if you are committed ///>> enough to take the journey of self-discovery and build a new life for yourself--a meaningful life in alignment with your purpose.

It's A Life-time of practices!

Reflection

Developing resilience

Developing resilience is a personal journey, and there are several different ways to building resilience. The following is a suggestion for how to approach life in a more positive way.

This exercise is about writing down things you are willing to do, to build your resilience, and create genuine happiness in your own life.

Journal

Get a journal, and write for few minutes every day, focusing on 3 things:

ex:

1 *--First, set your intention for that specific day. It could be being kind, listening with care, or hugging someone. Just choose one of the qualities from the Values list at the end of this book. Act on it during the day.*

P.115

2 *--Second, write the name of someone you care for, or a friend you want to keep in touch with, and give them a call during the day, send a caring message, or a text.*

3 ex *--Third, write about a nice thing you want to do for yourself that day, such as a walk in nature, listening to a nice song, reading a poem, or having a massage. It should be something to nurture yourself.*

You may think this is complicated, challenging, or useless. I thought so, too, when I initially began meditating every day (Mindfulness Meditation). There were times when I thought "this is futile, it is a waste of my time." It took six months before I really started feeling the difference in my own behavior, emotions, and body. Looking back, I realized that something small was changing every day but I could not see it.

Please remember that you are worthy of your own love and affection, and you have the privilege to share this love with the world.

Go ahead, get your journal, and start writing every day.

If you forget, it is normal and ok. Simply restart again, write every day and keep the intention alive in your mind and your heart.

If you reach a point of despair because you are not doing it perfectly, laugh at yourself for being so self-critical, and forgive yourself.

Be compassionate with yourself. (The circle of compassion is not complete unless you are in it).

You are only human, do the best you can.

Never give up.

Keep doing what you are doing, even if it does not make sense sometimes. Eventually it will.

Meditate and pray every day.

CHAPTER 6

GENUINE HAPPINESS

"Happiness is when you think, what you say, and what you do are in harmony."

-Mahatma Gandhi

The pursuit of happiness is one of your inalienable rights. One way to be happy is to find meaning in your work. It gives your life purpose. Most of us search for happiness in the external world, in a great relationship, a wonderful job, a beautiful home, a luxury car, or exotic vacations. We are looking for a stimulus- driven pleasure. In a TED talk, "The Surprising Science of Happiness," Dr. Dan Gilbert, PhD describes research that has shown external events such as winning the election, getting a promotion, or losing a romantic partner have a much less intense effect on us and a much shorter duration than we expect.

One model coming from this research states that outside circumstances in life are responsible for only 10% of our happiness, with 50% being genetically determined and 40% attributed to intentional activities such as thoughts, actions, and behaviors.

OUR happiness oRigins,

36

There is nothing wrong with working hard to get a good job, a better life, a loving relationship, and a nice home. It is just more important to do it with the right attitude and not get attached to the results. Attachment could be the cause of our suffering. When our thoughts and actions are in alignment with our values, as well as being beneficial to ourselves and others, we feel better. We need to realize that external things are impermanent, and if we want our happiness to last, we must do the things we feel good about, not only the things that make us feel good.

I have asked myself more than once: "Do I want to save the world or do I want to be happy?" Slowly, I realized that I cannot save the world. All I can do is focus on one person at a time, do the best I can with what I have, forgive myself for my shortcomings, help others, and strive to live according to my values in order to be genuinely happy.

We, as physicians, are workaholics, perfectionists, highly motivated, driven, and cannot afford mistakes. That's what makes us successful. But also, it is the major factor behind our high rate of burnout. Expecting everyone around us to be perfect and responding to our needs is a call for disaster.

Relearning to be happy is a process. It takes awareness, perseverance, and years of practice. It takes shifting our focus from our ego-driven activities and the "eight worldly concerns"--to our values and our "Authentic Self." The eight worldly concerns, as described in John Bruna's book, *The Wisdom of a Meaningful Life*, are: Gain v. Loss, Pleasure v. Pain, Praise v. Criticism, and Good reputation v. Bad reputation.

When we stop being afraid of losing what we have, stop depending on others to validate our progress, and search for genuine happiness instead of only stimulus-driven pleasures, then our life will become more rewarding and more successful.

Sometimes we get attached to external things, thinking that if we have them, our life will be perfect and fulfilled. However, we discover that the pleasure is temporary and dissipates with time.

Most people confuse stimulus-driven pleasures with genuine happiness. They are attached to outside pleasures, disregarding the feeling of having achieved something meaningful in line with their mission and inner purpose.

There is no perfect job. Most people strive to become the best in what they do and are competitive, perfectionists, and sometimes sacrifice their well-being for the approval of others. They forget that the reason for success is to reach their potential for happiness and wisdom, not only their potential to earn and acquire.

So how can we reach that potential and rekindle the joy of loving what we do and doing what we love?

Life is unpredictable and impermanent and time of death is uncertain. Therefore, contemplate about what would really be important at the time of death. Is it all the things we acquire, or is it the quality of time we spend with our loved ones and the service we perform to make someone else happy?

Consistently in my workshops, when participants are asked to share what they would do if they had only 24 hours to live, almost everyone wants to spend the time with their loved ones, their children, their family, and their friends.

Reflection

Ask yourself these questions, and answer them in your journal:

Am I happy and fulfilled?

What does it mean to be happy, for me?

Is my job giving me room to grow and flourish?

What makes me happy is...

What moves me is...

What inspires me is ...

The person I look up to is ...

To be more fulfilled in my job I need ...

CHAPTER 7

HEALTH AND HEALING

"It is impossible to heal the body without healing the soul"

- Socrates ●

We, physicians, feel responsible for the lives and well-being of our patients, carry their problems with us, analyze their results, question our decisions, perform procedures, and do that to the best of our ability for every patient. We have a pressure to succeed – a pressure to be perfect. We cannot envision failure, and when we face challenges, complications, or death, we are not taught how to deal with it.

We compete against each other, we struggle, and we compare ourselves to a standard which is so high that very few can attain. What is demanded of us is inhuman, and we still do our best to face the challenges and succeed at all odds.

And at what price? The price has been too high, from personal problems to family disintegration, drug abuse, suicide attempts, and burnout. If we cannot take care of ourselves, how do we expect to take care of our patients?

Health is not the absence of disease. We learn a lot about diseases in medical school and residency, how to diagnose them, and how to treat them. We learn to prescribe medications to patients to treat their disease, or do surgeries and procedures to diagnose and fix them.

We did not learn how to treat the person as a whole. We did not learn how to care and empathize, and we did not learn how to listen.

Health is the integration and balance between all levels of our being: physical, emotional, mental, and spiritual. Most physical illnesses have an emotional component associated with it. Research from Harvard Medical School showed that 50-75% of all visits to physicians have a psychosomatic component.

If we do not address the mental and emotional level, sometimes we cannot cure the physical. It is not necessary to do extensive psychotherapy, but recognizing that it is an important factor can make a difference in the appropriate referral.

I remember many of my morbidly obese patients suffered from low self-esteem in addition to their urological problems. They did not believe they were going to get better, had lost hope, and were not compliant with their treatments. If these kinds of beliefs and behavior are not addressed in an effective way by the appropriate person, their medical symptoms may never get better.

Everything in our body is interconnected. We may go on a diet, but if we do not exercise, change our lifestyle, address the emotional component which makes us overeat, recognize what kind of mental messages we're giving ourselves, and get a support system to help us achieve our goals, we will not be successful. That's why most of the diets in the market do not work.

What we need is a symbiotic relationship between all the levels of our being. We need to give ourselves positive messages--that we can care for ourselves effectively. To do this I believe that we need to ask for higher guidance to sustain our efforts.

Elizabeth's story (The power of listening)

In Urology, there is a disease called Interstitial Cystitis consisting of severe frequency, urgency, and chronic pelvic pain which sometimes is debilitating. In the past, it was dismissed and people were labeled as hypochondriacs. Slowly, urologists realized that it is real and it is a disease which is devastating for some patients.

One of my patients, Elizabeth, a 48-year-old woman, came to me with persistent debilitating lower abdominal and pelvic pain, severe frequency, and resistance to all types of treatment including laparoscopy and surgery in a 3-year duration.

All tests were normal and she could not work or hold a job. She could not go out, and she spent most of her time looking for the next bathroom. I asked her a simple question, "Do you have stress in your life?" She burst into tears and kept crying for a few minutes. Then, she told me her story: she said that she was the only caregiver of her disabled, special-needs, teenage child, whom she had taken care of his entire life. In addition, three years ago, her husband had had a stroke and she had also been taking care of him. She was exhausted and desperate because she had no help and no support system. She did not know what to do and was going from one doctor's office to the next looking for answers. She said she felt better after our encounter and thanked me for caring. She went on for 3 months without any pain for the first time in 3 years. All I did was listen and care.

We need to ask the right questions and listen. Listen carefully not only to what the patient is saying, but also to what they do not say: their attitude, their body language, their fears, and their doubts. We need to give them the chance to express themselves and reach their own healing mechanism. Norman Cousins said in his book *Anatomy of an Illness*—"each patient carries his own doctor inside of him."

What is Healing?

Healing is the restoration of wholeness and the meaning of purpose in one's life. It is the application of love to when one is hurt. Healing does not necessarily mean curing. We can heal and continue to care even if the cure is not there. Healing happens when illness becomes an opportunity for connection and personal growth.

Some individuals change in response to their illness and can achieve miraculous results. Bernie Siegel, M.D., describes exceptional cancer patients (ECaP) in his book *Love, Medicine and Miracles*.[8] He explained how some patients survived their terminal illness diagnoses and lived many years against all odds. He calls them "fighting spirits." These are the people who respond with a visceral "yes" when asked if they want to live to be one hundred years old. Usually 15-20% of an average audience responds with "yes," compared to only 5% in a room full of physicians. "It is a tragedy that so few doctors have the self-confidence necessary to motivate others to believe in the future, and care for themselves," Siegel said. I do not think I would have had my hand up for a positive response when he asked that question many years ago.

Carl Simonton, M.D., wrote in his book, *Getting Well Again*,[9] about the effects of emotions on our immune system and how unresolved emotional issues can cause cancer in certain individuals. He describes the work of LeShan[10], with over 500 cancer patients that he worked with and that their youth was marked by a feeling of isolation, neglect, and despair. He also talked about Caroline

Thomas, a psychologist at John Hopkins University, who followed medical students and evaluated their psychological profiles. Those who developed cancer saw themselves as having experienced a lack of closeness with their parents, seldom demonstrated emotions, and were generally low-gear. Carl Simonton and his wife, Stephanie (coauthor of the book), also demonstrated that relaxation and mental imagery are among the most valuable tools they have found to help patients learn to believe in their ability to recover from cancer.

We are not taught to be optimistic in medical school. Every disease has a certain percentage attached to the possibility of cure. But we are taught to tell the patient about their risk of recurrence and how the disease is going to affect their physical and mental health, their sex life, eating habits, pain control, percentage of mortality, and 5-year survival rate. Yes, all those things are important, but we also need to be human. We need to distribute hope as part of our mission and calling rather than only distributing drugs. Medicine is not only a science, but also an art—the art of healing.

Bernie Siegel said that as part of their training all doctors should be required to attend healing services. This would allow doctors to learn that they can help by simply listening or sharing on an emotional and spiritual level.

I remember during one session of a prostate cancer support group that I facilitated for more than ten years, one of my patients, who had a radical prostatectomy, said that the diagnosis of cancer had changed his priorities. Immediately after his surgery, he retired from his job, and took time off to spend with family, friends, and loved ones. He wanted to take advantage of the time he had left. He is still alive over twenty-three years later.

Rachel Naomi Remen, in her book *Kitchen Table Wisdom*[11] talks about the doctor who was faced with a terminally ill cancer patient and in the predicament of there being nothing more that he could do for her. With a trembling voice, he said to her, "Let us pray together." She immediately began to cry. While still holding his hand, she said to him, "That would be very wonderful, doctor." This was unfamiliar territory for him, but he had an incredible healing experience as a result.

So, yes, health and healing are interrelated. No more is it the dichotomy between science and art or science and spirituality which are both uniting to reclaim the real mission of our medical education, reclaim our right to care for our patient, listen to them, be compassionate, and heal them with love before we heal them with medications and procedures.

So, the burning questions need to be asked: "Are you under stress? What is really upsetting you? What kind of support do you need? What are your spiritual beliefs?" Every time I asked these questions of my patients it created a human connection beyond science and neutral interaction. It created the bond of healing.

Healing is mutual. We get healed by our patients like they get healed by us. They may give you a hug, a smile, or a warm handshake which will make your day and make the work you do worthwhile. In the long run we might say that the ultimate purpose of healing is to bring us closer to God.

In Bernie Siegel's book, *Peace, Love, and Healing*,[12] he asked two young, dying patients what message they wanted to send to young doctors on their graduation day. They had simple requests. One of them said, "tell them to let me talk first," while the other said, "tell them to knock on my door, say hello and goodbye, and look me in the eye when they talk to me." What an amazing message!

Listening compassionately with care will allow each patient to open up to their own healing mechanism and own healing resources.

CHAPTER 8

NEW MODEL MEDICINE

*"No matter how expert the physician is, if his/her
heart is not positive, then the physician's effectiveness is
lessened… The physician should show a genuine sense
of Care, Compassion, and concern. Then the patient
has more Hope and more Enthusiasm."*

-The Dalai Lama

As we learn to take care of ourselves, we can teach our patients
techniques for self-care. We shift to the era of new model medicine
where healing is shared, all caregivers do their part, and patients are
partners in the treatment decisions, understanding what is necessary
for their health and well-being. Patients care about themselves
enough to be motivated to make changes in lifestyle and health
habits. Patients access their own inner resources for healing as a
supplement to other forms of treatment.

Herbert Benson, from Harvard Medical School, compared health
and well-being to a three-legged stool. One leg is pharmaceutical,
one leg is surgery and procedures, and one leg is self-care. Health
and well-being are balanced and optimal when all three legs of the
stool are in place.

In my view, we need to add a fourth leg to the stool. It makes it more solid, more human, and more stable: The Leg of Compassionate Listening.

Listening compassionately with care will allow each patient to open up to their own healing mechanism and own healing resources.

Studies have shown that patients get interrupted by their doctors twenty-three seconds after they start talking. This was published in the *Journal of American Medical Association* (JAMA 1999). I do not think it has improved much currently. If anything, it is worse now with all the pressures and time constraints that providers are facing.

A patient needs a minimum of two minutes of uninterrupted conversation to feel heard. We need to reclaim the humanistic part of medicine and treat our patients like a whole spiritual person, not like a number or a disease. If we do not do this, then who will?

The focus of the 20th century has been on technology and outer space, with a separation between religion and science. The 21st century is reclaiming this relationship between spirituality and science, focusing on the inner space and the world within. The disappointments with violence, wars, greed, and callous disregard of people's lives have initiated many spiritual movements across the globe and have driven people to look within themselves for ways to understand and deal with life.

There is so much hunger in the world to bring spirituality into the mainstream. This hunger has affected medicine, as well. Because of the dominance of technology and paperwork replacing the human factor, this has created a general dissatisfaction with the care people are receiving from their physicians. The field of medicine has certainly made many advances scientifically: curing illnesses, extending lives, and using sophisticated technology. Unfortunately,

Assaad Mounzer, MD, MA, ACC, FACS

however, medicine has lost some of its most healing and positive attributes. Primarily, it has lost its ability to touch people's lives with compassion and empathy.

Larry Dossey, M.D., an international speaker and writer, in his book *Reinventing Medicine*[13] he defines this new era in medicine as Era III, which complements Era I and II to make it whole.

Era I is conventional medicine, Era II is mind-body medicine, and Era III would be spirituality and the human consciousness in medicine. He said, "People everywhere are starved for meaning, purpose, and spiritual fulfillment in their lives."

The purpose of life, from my point of view, is to show compassion, love, and kindness to ourselves and others, as well as to grow in wisdom. We need to listen to our patients, our friends, and our loved ones, make them partners in the decision, teach them how to find their inner healing mechanism, and learn the relaxation response (R-R), so when they are under stress they can elicit positive emotions and use the R-R for the healing of their heart, body, and immune system.

Herbert Benson and Jon Kabat-Zinn have found that the relaxation response and mindfulness-based stress reduction could be used to stabilize and decrease high blood pressure, treat chronic back pain, and decrease anxiety and stress in different settings.

Self-care includes practices on all levels: Physical, Mental, Emotional, Social and Spiritual, as explained in chapter 4. p. 17
p. 99

Reflection

How do we elicit the <u>Relaxation Response?</u> Do the following exercise:
<u>Chose a comfortable, private space. Sit with your back straight. Focus
on your breathing.</u>

<u>On the Physical level:</u>

- <u>Relax your muscles and release the tension.</u> Start at the top of
  your head, relaxing your forehead, the muscles around the eyes,
  your jaw muscles, and progressively go down to your neck, back,
  arms, and hands, then pelvis, thighs, legs and feet.
- <u>Invite your breathing to become slow</u> (diaphragmatic).
- Focus on the <u>belly expanding with inhalation</u> and relaxing
  <u>with exhalation.</u>
- <u>Results: Metabolism decreases.</u>
- <u>Heart rate and blood pressure decrease.</u>

<u>Mental level:</u>

- Observing and <u>letting go of thoughts</u>
- <u>No judgment</u>
- <u>No attachment</u>
- <u>Neutrality</u>
- <u>Gentleness</u>
- Give yourself permission to <u>release all concerns and anxieties</u>
  about the past or the future.

- *Results: Attention is turned inward with concentration on each breath.*
- *Observing/witnessing the arising and passing of thoughts, feelings, and sensations.*

If your mind wanders, it is no problem. Simply bring your focus back to each breath and develop an attitude of acceptance toward whatever happens in the process. Develop kindness and acceptance toward yourself.

CHAPTER 9

WHAT IS MINDFULNESS?

"Mindfulness is consciously attending to the present moment with wisdom and clarity and initiating actions in alignment with our values"

p115 -John Bruna

Mindfulness is becoming very popular these days to relieve stress, stabilize emotions, control pain, treat hyperactivity in schools, and build resilience for physicians.

DEF:
It has been defined as moment-by-moment, (non-judgmental) awareness of our thoughts, emotions, and bodily sensations. It is an intentional strategy of living. It includes attentive observation, critical curiosity, beginner's mind, acceptance, and presence.

Jon Kabat Zinn, in his book, *Wherever You Go There You Are*, defines it as the awareness that arises out of paying attention on purpose in the present moment and without judgment. He goes on to say that mindfulness has to do, above all, with attention, awareness, being fully awake and perceiving the exquisite vividness of each moment.

In his book, *The Wisdom of a Meaningful Life*,[14] John Bruna describes Mindfulness Practice as much more than a present moment awareness. He explains that there are four key points to Mindfulness Practice: attention, values, wisdom, and an open heart. Without these key points, mindfulness would be just another form of meditation.

One of the biggest obstacles to finding inner peace and developing our highest potential is our untrained mind. The mind continuously produces thoughts and images and compulsively draws our attention away from what we are doing. We need to train our mind to be present and to attend to what we choose, rather than having it constantly dragging us around. "Honkey" mind

The practice of mindfulness brings relaxation to the body, clarity to the mind, and stability to the emotions. We become more aware of the actions that lead to the suffering of one's self and others and choose consciously to shift our attention and to act accordingly. This is how we acquire wisdom. To experience genuine happiness, we need to choose our positive values to guide our intention every morning and then decide how we want to show up in the world.

Finally, open-heartedness is an essential key to mindfulness practice and genuine happiness. By cultivating the attitudes of equanimity, loving kindness, compassion, and empathetic joy, we consciously water the flowers instead of the weeds in our thoughts and actions.

Mother Teresa did not have much, but she had one of the most valuable qualities in human life: compassion. She fed the hungry, comforted the rejected, and sat with sick people at hospitals doors, holding them in her arms until the door of the hospital opened to receive them or until they died. She did not have to fix them, she just loved them. She was one of the happiest people on this earth and that earned her the privilege to become a Saint.

How are we sure that mindfulness works to build resilience and avoid burnout? p29

The University of Rochester School of Medicine demonstrated that mindful practice helped physicians and health professionals enhance their self-awareness, wellness, and resilience, improve their relationships with patients and colleagues, and advance the quality of medical care they provide.

Colin West, MD, and his colleagues[15], reviewed 2617 articles – 15 of them being randomized trials and 37 being cohort studies, which were of sufficient quality, including their own research at Mayo Clinic. These studies concluded that interventions reduced overall burnout, as well as emotional exhaustion and depersonalisation. The interventions included mindfulness, discussion groups, and stress management.

Krasner, MD, demonstrated that intensive educational programs in mindfulness, communication, and self-awareness are associated with improvement in primary care physicians' well-being and a decrease in burnout and psychological distress.[16] The intervention consisted of 8 weekly, 2.5-hour sessions, plus an all-day (7 hour) silent retreat, and a maintenance phase (10 monthly, 2.5-hour sessions) where participants engaged in mindful meditations, awareness of thoughts and feelings, explored self-care, reflected on meaningful experiences in their practice, and examined end-of-life care.

p29

This program has shown to build resilience and cut down on the percentage of burnout. They stressed the point of bringing together three clinical issues in healthcare: quality, cost, and the well-being of the clinician workforce. They encouraged the formation of resilience-promoting programs to build community among clinicians and other members of the healthcare workforce. "Just as patient safety is the responsibility of communities of practice, so is clinician well-being and support", the study reported.

The mindful communication program's results from Mayo Clinic showed sustained improvement in physicians' well-being and quality of patient care, in addition to increased emotional stability of physicians. What also struck them when they interviewed the physician participants, were two unexpected findings: their need for a community (because physicians felt a sense of isolation) and their ability to give themselves permission to engage in activities to improve self-care and self-awareness.

In the present moment, we need to pay attention--with wisdom and clarity and without judgment--to our thoughts, emotions, and activities. We need to have clear intentions and initiate actions in alignment with our values. *P.98*

CHAPTER 10

NEUROPLASTICITY

"All emotions are healthy, because emotions are what unite the mind and the body. Anger, fear, sadness, the so-called negative emotions are as healthy as peace, courage and joy."

-Candace Pert

The brain is a very complex organ, with 100 billion neurons (nerve cells). It has a great capacity to adapt to different stressful situations as well as different kinds of traumas, whether physical, emotional, or social. The triune brain theory explains that there are three layers to the human brain:

*The brainstem—which controls the flow of messages between the brain and the rest of the body and is responsible for breathing, excretion, blood flow, body temperature and other autonomic functions like the fight or flight response.

*The limbic system—which encircles the top of the brainstem and is the seat of the emotions. It works closely with the brainstem and body to create our emotions and basic drives.

3 (*The cerebral cortex—located in the forebrain and which is the seat of reason and critical thinking.

The brain can form new connections and new circuits to relearn certain activities and certain other physical and mental abilities. This happens, for example, when someone has a stroke or paralysis. With re-education and practice some of the functions can be restored. Neuroplasticity allows the neurons in the brain to compensate for injury and disease by "axonal sprouting." The intact axons grow new nerve endings to reconnect neurons which are damaged, and to adjust their activities in response to new situations or to changes in their environment.

Neuroplasticity can also occur with behavior, environmental stimuli, thought, and emotions which have significant implications for healthy development, learning, memory, and recovery from brain damage.

Research in the field of Neuroscience shows that we can create new neural pathways, neural connections, and change our brain with our intentional activities. The Hebbian Theory states that "Neurons that fire together, wire together, and neurons that fire out of sync, fail to link."

One of the key practical lessons of modern neuroscience is that the power to direct our attention has within it the power to shape our brain's firing patterns as well as the power to shape the architecture of the brain itself.

"What we attend to becomes our reality," Richard Davidson says by popularizing the idea that one can learn happiness and compassion as skills just as one learns to play a musical instrument or train oneself in sports such as golf or tennis.

Davidson[17] discovered that people who are resilient (able to regain their emotional balance after a setback rather than wallowing in anxiety, anger, depression, or another negative emotion) have strong connections between the left prefrontal cortex (PFC) and the amygdalae. The left PFC sends inhibitory signals to the amygdalae, essentially telling them to quiet down.

We know that mindfulness can improve mental functions, relieve anxiety, pain, and make people more relaxed and focused. We did not have the scientific proof until a few years ago through the work of Sara Lazar and her associates.

Sara Lazar, PhD, a Harvard Neuroscientist, used an MRI to look at brain activity in fine detail to show that meditation could promote neural plasticity and that it may also be associated with structural changes in areas of the brain that are important for sensory, cognitive, and emotional processing.

Another study by Lazar and Holzel [18] concluded that meditation could produce a thickening in four areas of the brain after eight weeks of mindfulness meditation. One of the important areas is the temporo-parietal junction, which is associated with empathy, compassion, self-awareness, adaptability, self-motivation, emotional balance, and social grace – all great qualities of emotional intelligence. A 2013 University of Illinois study looked at various brain areas activated during emotional intelligence-centered activities like social interaction. Their finding was amazing. The researchers identified one particular region, the temporo-parietal junction (TPJ), to be prominently "lit up" on the brain scan images.

Another area which lit up on MRI screens was the prefrontal cortex, which is the center of awareness, concentration, and decision-making. This was the part of the brain which was very developed in Einstein's brain. Increased thickness in this "king of all brain

pre frontal Cortex

regions" means many great things: far less anxiety and depression, stronger willpower, more success, more processing power, and better health.

The studies by Lazar also show a reduction in volume of the amygdala. Participants reported reduction in stress which was also correlated with decreased grey-matter density in the amygdala, which is known to play an important role in anxiety and stress.

Therefore, it turns out, that "we can teach an old dog new tricks." (p.98) With intentional activity, like concentration, meditation and mindfulness, we can rewire our brain, creating new neural pathways that promote mental and emotional balance. This allows us to continue to learn, grow, and develop new healthy habits at any age. And we may also sleep better and live longer. If you still feel tired, drowsy, and fatigued after lying in bed all night, you are likely not getting enough deep, quality sleep. Spending sufficient time in the REM stage is critical to your mental, emotional and physical well-being. Neuroscientists have discovered that mindfulness builds up the size of the Pons, at the base of the brain, which regulates the main dreamtime chemical: melatonin.

One of the key practical lessons of modern neuroscience is that the power to direct our attention has within it the power to shape our brain's firing patterns as well as the power to shape the architecture of the brain itself

More research has shown that there is a change in gene expression with regular meditation and mindfulness practice. Telomeres grow stronger and longer, correlating with an increased life span. Telomeres are protective DNA and protein complexes at the end of linear chromosomes that promote chromosomal stability.

Telomere shortness in human beings is a prognostic marker of aging, disease and premature morbidity. Dean Ornish and colleagues found that comprehensive lifestyle intervention (Stress management, diet, exercise, and social support) was associated with significant increases in relative telomere length after five years of follow up, compared with controls (active surveillance alone) in men with biopsy-proven low risk prostate cancer.

Reflection

Mindfulness Practice: P 5)

First, let us start with a meditation practice every morning. Begin with 10 minutes and slowly increase to 24 minutes a day.

Choose a consistent, comfortable place, preferably in the morning, before the distractions of the day begin. Focus on your breathing. Feel your belly expand when you inhale and retract when you exhale. Feel the sensation of each breath filling your lungs and then released. Ride your breath--in and out....

Mentally surround yourself with a healing white light for protection and according to your spiritual or religious beliefs. Then, scan your body slowly--from the top of your head to your toes. Be aware of every muscle--open your forehead, soften the area around the eyes, relax the jaw while also keeping a focus on your belly expanding with each inhalation. Let the healing light of awareness slowly move down to your neck and shoulders. If there is any tightness, send some love, warmth, and relaxation to each area that feels tense. Continue the same process with your arms, hands, back, legs and feet.

This is a concentration meditation with the purpose of training your mind to focus and pay attention to each breath. Eventually this practice will help you learn to start paying attention to your daily intention, and what is important to you during daily activities.

P98

Meditation is only a small part of mindfulness practice. The bulk of your practice is in how you live your life, says John Bruna. Bringing your attention back to the breath will focus the monkey mind to the object of awareness that you choose.

It takes a significant amount of time to build and perfect this practice. If your mind wanders, acknowledge the thoughts and bring your attention back to the breath. Keep your mind alert. If your mind wanders fifty times and you bring it back fifty times to the breath, these are fifty mindful moments.

After your body relaxes and your mind is clear and focused, set your intentions for your day. Choose one value you want to focus on and keep track of it with a daily mindfulness sheet (see the page for this sheet at the end of the book). P 112

Keep repeating to yourself: "May I be …(insert your quality or intention).

Every time you catch yourself doing an unskillful action, just write it down. It is an observation – no need to do anything else. If you catch yourself doing something good, in alignment with your intention and your values, document that as well.

In the evening, review your day-- with acceptance and no judgment. Know that it is never going to be perfect. We are all human beings and we repeatedly make the same mistakes (or "unskillful actions"). The key is to forgive ourselves and to use our wisdom and discerning awareness to do better the next time.

P 112   P 51, P 110

[The Daily Mindfulness Sheet, and Daily Practice Sheet are at the end of this book for you to use and convenience.]

- Reflection
- meditation
- mindfulness

CHAPTER 11

MY TRANSFORMATION WITH COACHING AND MINDFULNESS. P 51

"Awake at dawn with a winged heart, and give thanks for another day of loving."

-Khalil Gibran

What is coaching? It is partnering with you, the client, in a thought-provoking and creative process that inspires you to maximize your personal and professional potential.

Coaching is a sacred relationship. It is a process of self-discovery to guide you to your inner wisdom. It will help you understand stress and how it affects your life, clarify your path, help you trust your instincts, and proactively create and sustain the life you want.

Coaching includes active listening, direct communication, and creating awareness to allow you to design actions and promote progress in your personal and professional life. It is about appreciating yourself for everything you are doing, get personal validation for helping people, and find more meaning and fulfillment in your work.

How did I get into coaching? I wanted to prepare myself for a retirement job – one without stress – and by exploring different options I found coaching ideal for me, especially with my background in psychology. So, I obtained the certification and it was an amazing discovery. What I discovered is what coaching could offer to people in a very loving and supportive environment. Specifically: confidentiality without the pressure of providing solutions.

While preparing for my certification with ICF (International Coach Federation), where I am now a member, I continued exploring the burnout phenomena which is spreading like cancer into our healthcare profession. No one is talking about it or seemingly even aware of the damage it can do. I found out that there are many external and internal factors to burnout and different organizations and associations should address the external factors and create a friendlier and more supportive environment for their employees and their physicians and providers. The internal factors are for us to deal with.

P 5/

I took the mindfulness training myself in order to get certified as a teacher. During this journey I found out that it is an amazing tool for me to help me become present and more aware of my emotions and thoughts. It also helped me establish a life in alignment with my values and purpose. We are all talented people and the world needs us to make a positive difference in our lives and the lives of others when we can. Simultaneously, we need to exercise our right to be happy and joyful.

I was so grateful for this training. I learned that what makes me really happy is to have my family around me, feeling the love and support of my wife and children, and also being there for them.

Keeping in touch with my mother and brother and my extended family, as well as good friends, is enough for me to regenerate my energy and enthusiasm. I learned that my possessions are an important part of my comfort-life and that I worked hard for them, so it is legitimate for me to enjoy them. At the same time, I realized that getting attached to possessions and the external things is not healthy and only produces suffering, especially since it can generate a never-ending cycle of wanting more. So, creating that balance is essential for me to stay genuinely happy.

During this practice, I saw myself becoming more compassionate, more present, and more focused. My emotions became increasingly balanced and my thoughts, of course, were still racing, but learning to refocus my attention to what I really want was more fulfilling. Exercising the breathing meditation every day, and cultivating my attention to come back to the breath every time my mind wandered, was a great tool to help me remain focused during the day on my intention and my values. It does not mean I never partake in wasteful actions, get angry or resentful, or show hate or envy, but it makes me more aware of these actions so that I can refocus my attention to the intention of that day and the values I want to live by.

P·a8   P 115

It took six months of daily practice, with doubts and negative thoughts, constantly wondering if I was doing the right thing in order to realize that I *was* making progress.

It was not until one day when I was visiting my mom in Lebanon and everyone who visited us from our neighborhood made the observation that I looked very peaceful. It dawned on me then that I really was more peaceful and that I could not even remember the last time I had gotten angry.

Slowly, I found myself stopping before reacting in an angry or resentful way and taking a few seconds to decide how I wanted to answer, I changed my behavior in a way consistent with my intention for the day. What an amazing way to feel good about oneself and to accept things as they are without judgment or resentment and to take the next step in my growth and fulfillment. This happened many times and now it is becoming a natural way of life and happens automatically even before I think about it.

New habits take time to get anchored in our consciousness and eventually they replace our old habits. I also found that mindfulness helped me in my coaching practice. It helped me become more present, more confident, and more expressive in my compassion, with caring and detachment. Detachment does not mean indifference. *Def!* Quite the contrary. It means understanding and being willing to help without getting entangled in the emotions of the client.

Dr. Marcia Reynolds (PsyD, MCC) one of the top master coaches in the world, said, "If you use self-awareness and maintain a confident and caring presence, empathy will help you be a more effective leader and coach" (LinkedIn July 9, 2017).

As said before, there is empathy fatigue but not compassion fatigue. When you take on other people's feelings and live their experience, it can make you susceptible to depression and hopelessness. Compassion, on the contrary, will give you hope and enthusiasm because you know you have the power to do something about it--just by listening and understanding. No need to fix or cure, but instead just show loving and listen with compassion.

My experience with Mindfulness has been very rewarding. Now I am a certified MLP mindfulness teacher. I facilitate workshops for Mindfulness practice and Mindfulness based stress reduction. I teach the Foundations course for mindfulness as it was taught to me during my MLP certification.

p 51

The Foundations course is an eight week course with one specific subject for every week. It starts with being aware of our obsessive and delusional mind, to learn attention and intentional practice, to determine the difference between genuine happiness and stimulus driven pleasure. It progresses to an understanding of our emotions, how to make our relationships better, and how to use our wisdom in order to live a meaningful life in alignment with our values. During the training, we watch different TED talks videos relevant to the keys of Mindfulness.

We participate in rich discussions and sharing.

Every time, we practice a different kind of meditation. Breathing meditation. Loving kindness meditation. Grounding meditation. The three-thoughts meditation. And the transforming unskillful events meditation. Also, we practice different kinds of indoors and outdoors mindfulness activities. Join us in our workshops, we will listen to you with loving and compassion, treat you like dear friends, and support you in any way we can. Check our website: www.mindfulmdcoaching.com

Testimonials from people who took the training:

> *"This training has been life-changing for me. Something as simple as breathing, increasing awareness, and empathy on a daily basis can lead to contentment and less stress. A Winning Program!"*

-Maria. Z. Associate professor, at Bluefield College

> *"This course was a true banquet of knowledge and practice. I am hungry for more".*

-Kathleen. M., Mindfulness participant

"I learned that I am the only person who can make me happy. I need to remind myself daily of the things that bring me genuine happiness"

-L. M., Mindfulness participant

"This training has helped me determine priorities in my life and to evaluate why I feel so stressed. It has helped me to remember my values and that I cannot care for my family if I do not take care of myself"

-Susan. G., Director B. Clinic

[Check our website for the schedule of our activities at: www. mindfulmdcoaching.com]

Meditations:
1) Loving Kindness
2) Grounding
3) Breathing

CHAPTER 12

PSYCHO-NEURO-IMMUNOLOGY

"We know that the immune system, like the central nervous system, has memory and the capacity to learn. Thus, it could be said that intelligence is located not only in the brain but in cells that are distributed throughout the body, and that the traditional separation of mental processes, including emotions, from the body is no longer valid."

-Candace Pert

The term Psychoneuroimmunology (PNI) was introduced by American psychologist Robert Ader in 1981 to describe the study of interactions between psychological, neurological and immune systems. There is evidence supporting the brain and central nervous system's influence to enhance immune function and improve our health.

Do you remember when you were a child and got hurt and just a kiss from your mom made the pain go away? How do you explain that?

It is the effect of the Endorphins (one of the neurotransmitters from our brain), or Endogenous morphine, which are secreted and have the beneficial effect of pain control, much like Dopamine which energizes us as a kind of the placebo effect.

Our body is rich in Neurotransmitters. They are the messengers of our thoughts and emotions. We call them the "Psychosomatic communication network."

Neurotransmitters are Neuropeptides--small protein-like molecules (made of amino acids) used by our Neurons to communicate with each other and with the rest of the body. They are involved in a wide range of brain functions, including metabolism, social behaviors, learning, and memory. Neuropeptides modulate neuronal communication by acting on cell surface receptors.

Candace Pert, a neuroscientist at Harvard and author of the book *Molecules of Emotions*[19], said, "if the cell is the engine that drives all life, then the receptors are the buttons on the control panel of that engine, and a specific peptide is the finger that pushes that button and gets things started."

Neurotransmitters are responsible for keeping us alive. Humans have around 100 different peptides in our bodies, encoded by 90 genes. The most prominent are Dopamine, Norepinephrine, Epinephrine (or Adrenaline), Acetylcholine, Histamine, Serotonin, and Enkephalin (5 amino acids long) or Endorphins. Endorphins do not only exist in the brain. New discoveries found that they are also in the immune system, the endocrine system, and other areas in our bodies.

When Candace Pert discovered the opiate receptors, it started a revolution that created profound shifts within nearly every field of modern medicine. It united immunology, endocrinology, neurophysiology, psychology and biology into a discipline called Psychoneuroimmunology (PNI) which was the beginning for a cohesive theory about how our thoughts and emotions are capable of creating wellness or diseases in our body.

Emotions are not only psychological, they are also chemical in that they affect the chemicals in our brain. We can affect our own emotions, with intentional practices, which explains why meditation and the relaxation response work as well as developing positive affirmations and positive visualizations.

Many people can use visualization to control their disease, lower their high Blood pressure and even destroy cancer cells, curing themselves from cancer. Although it happens rarely, there are a lot of reports in the literature about spontaneous remission of cancer, where patients worked on themselves with visualization, prayer and faith to induce wellness.

Each one of us has the power to heal. We must trust the wisdom of our cells. If, with our mind, we can create illness (psychosomatic diseases), we can also create wellness and health. With strong enough beliefs, we can remember wellness.

 A thought can create the same reaction as reality in the brain. Our mind is in every cell of our body. As soon as the transmitters are released and interact with the receptors, our body knows what to do immediately and reacts in a specific way.

For example, if you remember a delicious dessert and imagine yourself eating it again, your salivary glands will start secreting, your stomach acidity increases and you may get hungry. Another example is when you remember a sexual or erotic encounter and you imagine yourself involved with it, your body will get aroused automatically and vaginal secretions may increase or erection may happen as if it was happening in the present.

[If you want to check our library for positive visualizations, check our website: www.mindfulmdcoaching.com ✗

You will find CDs for: Improving your immune system.

Healing your heart

Preparation for surgery.]

p.70 | Released
transmitter ⟶ acts w/ the receptors ⟶
↗ body Reacts in a certain way.

p.69 Cell ⟶ receptors ⟶ neuro peptide ⟶
body Reaction

Reflection

Exercise:

Be good to yourself and start your personal healing program.

Write down here an affirmation starting with " I am" and add the actions and values that are important to you, the goals you want to achieve, and phrase it as if it has already happened.

In other words it is a positive visualization showing that you have already achieved what you want.

5

A good affirmation has five basic ingredients:

It is personal. It starts with I am…

It is positive.

It is present tense.

It is visual (see yourself achieving the result)

It is emotional (it has a deep meaning for you).

Examples of affirmations:

"I am a wise man using my loving kindness and compassion to make a difference in my life and the lives of the people I touch."

"I am healthy in mind, body and spirit, exercising regularly, eating healthy, and am optimistic about the future. I am wealthy and happy in all ways."

"I am achieving my goals in a timely manner--with excellence, ease and grace."

Now, write your affirmation on several cards and put them in places where you can see them every day--on your sink, in your car, in your office, etc...

This will help you in achieving your goals. Remember, too, the Self-Care List you started in chapter 4 to take care of yourself on all levels (physical, mental, emotional and spiritual), and practice them every day.

P 17

Change the goals if you have to, and make them achievable. Once you reach one goal, it improves your self-esteem and gives you the energy and motivation to go for the next goal.

Have faith and know that all will happen at the right time, for your highest good and the highest good of all concerned.

CHAPTER 13

DISCUSSION GROUPS

"The important thing is this: to be able at any moment to sacrifice what we are for what we would become"

-Charles Du Bos

We have learned that by practicing mindfulness we build resilience, and strengthen our ability to bounce back. We find meaning in our work by taking actions in alignment with our values, and by keeping an open heart and having a support group. Research from Mayo clinic with physicians, shows that protected time (60 minutes every two weeks) in small facilitated discussion groups (6-8), resulted in increased meaning and reduced depersonalization and burnout.

Follow-up data found sustained benefits at one year after the close of the study. The value and benefits for these physicians included developing and maintaining a personal sense of covenant and service, supporting and validating the interactional values of medicine that give meaning to the physician's work, and strengthening the physician's commitment while activating more of these values in patient relationships. It also strengthened their sense of personal calling and spiritual community within the medical system, as well as their individual capacity to see meaning in each patient's story.

It created safe, nonjudgmental, and non-competitive interactions among colleagues.

Physicians, nationwide, are developing self-directed and on-going values and meaning, as well as study groups in their communities and at their medical centers independent of institutional support. Participating physicians become resources for one another.

Finding meaning in (medicine) groups could be done in the following way:

Each evening will have a topic that is decided by the group in the previous session. Everyone shares their stories and thoughts and the group responds openly to what they have heard. A safe, nonjudgmental, and non-competitive interaction between participants is encouraged.

Each person could bring a story about a dying friend or patient, for example, and how it has affected them, or they might bring a meaningful poem to read and discuss with the group. This enables them to explore these topics in greater depth.

Topics could consist of suffering and loss, grief, awe in medicine, fear, surrender, forgiveness and mistakes, compassion, and service.

Ground rules could include: confidentiality (which is essential to create a safe space); respect for each other's opinions; no criticism and no advice giving and only sharing of personal experiences, allowing time for each person to share.

We conducted a 6-week course, 2 1/2 hours for each meeting, for the residents at our hospital. We followed the curriculum of the "Healer's Art," as described by R. N. Remen, MD, when she started it at UC San Francisco many years ago, which has been adopted by many medical schools around the country. The program consists of sharing with each other, discussing difficulties, losses, and grief, and remembering the awe that brought us to medicine in the first place while, again, finding meaning in what we do on a daily basis.

Listed here are some of the evaluations of the residents:

"I learned to *focus on myself for* improvement and incorporate into life the things I love and enjoy."

"I was able to identify times in my life when I was *calm and at peace.*"

"Seeing others struggle with the same problems is encouraging in a sense; *it helps knowing I am not the only one*"

"It helped me realize what I need in my life to help me *feel safe and secure.*"

"I learned that it is ok *to take time for myself to nurture my own spirit and mind.*"

"I felt I was *not alone feeling the way I do.*"

"I learned to trust my peers as they are, *as they have gone through the same stuff as I did.*"

"Life is not all about work. *I rekindled my lost love of being creative.*"

"*I learned that I forgot who I was* before medical school. It brought back things that are important to me."

Reflection

Support groups are beneficial for everyone, not only physicians.

Start a support group for yourself. Hang out with people who are positive and who have the same values you have. Decide to meet on a regular basis-- once a week or once every two weeks-- to do an activity you like, such as: play tennis, write poetry, go for a hike in nature, start a book club, or just sit down and talk sharing your feelings or challenges.

Be careful that this time is not spent giving advice to each other or to solve problems or play the victim. It is about listening actively and having an open ear to listen to others and for others to listen to you with an open heart and no judgment.

Sometimes it is helpful to choose a subject in advance. You can take turns picking the subject of these discussions, which might include: relationships, about grief or loss, about diet, exercise classes, or even golf scores. Bring pictures, articles, poems, or even movies to watch and discuss. Have fun with it. This is a time for bonding, fellowship and friendship.

Be dynamic, and flexible and open to others joining your group. Be sure to establish some guidelines like confidentiality, informing others if you cannot make it, listening with respect, allowing silence, sharing only your personal experience, etc...

Everyone needs a friend who listens to you and shares their own ideas and feelings. There is so much hunger in the world for connection, intimacy and compassionate listening.

CHAPTER 14

COMPASSIONATE LISTENING: THE FOURTH LEG OF THE STOOL

"True compassion does not come from wanting to help those less fortunate than ourselves, but from realizing our kinship with all beings."

-Pema Chodron

Listening is what we often do least. Most of us are anxious to give our opinion, share our experiences, and show off our knowledge. We want to be admired, appreciated, and acknowledged. We go from one person to another looking for approval and anxious to hear even a word of gratitude.

We use social media – jump from Facebook to Twitter to LinkedIn – and we like it when others "Like" us and share our posts. We want to reach as many people as we can and to have many friends. But at the end of the day we are left alone with our iPhone wondering where all those friends really are. Why don't they call me to talk to me? Why don't they meet me for coffee so we can have a face-to-face interaction? People are desperate to be heard and to be validated so they can feel good about themselves.

How much do we listen? Unfortunately, most of us have lost the ability to listen and to be silent.

LISTEN
SILENT

Did you notice that these words have the same letters? When the placement of the letters is changed, listen becomes silent. To hear others, we must be still, open our ears and hearts, and quiet our mind. We must get rid of the chatter and listen with intent, silence, and with love and empathy.

There is no need to fix anything, but rather just understand, create a safe space, and embrace the suffering of the other person.

We hold a lot of tension in our body manifested as unexpressed grief and sadness. Sometimes our friends and even our patients come to us with a myriad of symptoms, the least of them sometimes being what they originally came for. Here is an exemplary story of one of my patients.

Ralph's story

I remember a patient of mine, whom we will call Ralph here. Ralph came to me with pain and swelling everywhere, but mainly in his genital area and legs. He had just gotten out of the hospital where I saw him for the first time when he had a bad infection.

He was very frustrated when he came to my office for a follow up visit. He said there was not much improvement in his condition and he was angry that no one could do anything for him. I listened to him, but there was not much I could recommend. His symptoms were going to take time to resolve and I was wondering how I could help him. Just before he left the office, I asked him: "What are you angry about?"

He gave me a sad look and told me that he lost his twenty-year-old son two years ago to a car accident and had never had the time to grieve. He started to cry and apologized for it, saying that this was the first time he had cried about it because he wanted to be strong for his wife and did not want anyone to see him cry. In a way, he felt ashamed. I told him that it was ok to cry. He was sobbing, so I gave him a big hug and stayed with him until he calmed down. He felt better and I could see a softening in his face which now looked more relaxed. He thanked me before he left--for listening and caring.

I was happy to be able to witness the relief for at least part of his suffering; especially since he had kept it bottled up for two years. I am sure, now, that this will help him heal in a more effective way. Compassion is not about suffering with people, it is about acknowledging their suffering and doing the best we can to help alleviate it.

The world is hungry for people who listen, understand, and care. People are desperate to be heard; if only we were to give them the chance-- just a few moments of our life – real caring moments.

I understood at that point what compassion was. It is much more powerful than empathy. Empathy is when we can walk a mile in someone else's shoes and feel their pain and struggle to make them feel better, yet are unable to be real effective in that way. This action can create empathy fatigue and burnout.

Compassion is when we understand someone else's pain and can relieve their suffering with a word, a touch, or just a listening ear. There is no such things as "compassion fatigue." On the contrary, compassion gives us the chance to experience genuine happiness because we had the chance to be with someone else in a positive way. In this sense it actually gives us more energy.

As Bernie Siegel said, "Truth without compassion is hostility."

We can give a patient the bad news of their having cancer and instead of leaving the room, we can wait for them to assimilate and integrate the idea. This is devastating news for someone and they may choose to be in denial for a while or to get angry or to start crying. We have to be compassionate enough to stay with them at these times and to see them cry, and hold their hand if needed and tell them that we understand and will do what we can to relieve their suffering.

Sometimes emotional suffering is even more devastating than the physical pain. People worry about things such as their loved ones, about medical costs, about their ability to cope, and about having a support system.

Most of us physicians did not learn about compassion in medical school. Most of us feel uncomfortable if a patient starts to cry, and we leave the room or call the nurse for support. This is unfortunate and it is one of the reasons why 55% of physicians have symptoms of burnout.

As I said in chapter 8 on new model medicine," we have to add a fourth leg to the caregiver's stool. Herbert Benson described health care as a three legged stool, one leg being medications, one leg being procedures, and one leg being Self-Care. Here, I am adding a fourth leg: the Leg of Compassionate Listening.

Listening compassionately with care will allow each patient to open up to their own healing mechanism and own healing resources. It makes the stool more solid, more human, and more stable.

When we are faced with life and death decisions, major problems to solve, or complex issues to be resolved, it is very easy to feel the effects of burnout. As physicians, we are experiencing that every day and if we do not care for ourselves we are going to experience burnout. Instead, we need to remember to include ourselves in the circle of compassion.

More than 70% of Americans turn to alternative and complementary Medicine for a relief of their symptoms because they are finding there an ear that listens. People want to find someone who empowers them and gives them the kind of hope that allows them to get over their obstacles. Hope gives a boost to their immune system and empowers them to take initiative and learn how to care for themselves. They start being a partner in their own health, and not simply feeling as if they are simply victims.

In his book *Spiritual Awakening,*[20] Elder Paisios, a Christian Greek Orthodox monk and saint from Mount Athos, said: "When the doctors and nurses feel genuine compassion for their patients, this is the most effective medicine. The patients feel they are being cared for with love and have a sense of certainty, security, and consolation." He continued to say that compassion, love and service provide great spiritual strength.

CHAPTER 15

THE BURDEN OF WORRYING

I remember when I was in Lebanon between 2004 and 2006, I had a small office in my hometown where I saw patients once a week. I wanted that to be a gift for the people I cherish and love in the town I grew up in. It gave me a lot of satisfaction to be able to be of service. Here is a story taken from those years and that experience.

Sophie's story

One of the first patients I saw in this office in Lebanon was Sophie, a young 16-year-old girl who came with her mother and little brother. She was quiet and innocent, spoke with a soft voice, and started telling me about her symptoms of urgency and frequency which was interrupted several times by her mother who was very concerned about her stomach problems. She said Sophie had been hospitalized several times for diarrhea and abdominal pain. She had been taking medication for two years, almost daily, to no avail.

Intuitively I asked the girl, "What is bothering you at school?" She smiled and I saw tears in her eyes. I knew there was something more she wanted to tell me. I waited. Her mother intervened and said, "She worries about us a lot!"

"What do you mean?" I replied. The mother said: "Since her brother died seven years ago, she has not been the same." I was devastated to listen to the rest of the story and had tears in my eyes during the whole visit.

Sophie had lost her brother who was electrocuted at home. She did not feel responsible for his death, but she had been worried sick about her four other brothers who are all younger than her. Her father had left two years before to go to another country to work, leaving Sophie and her mother with the responsibility of taking care of the rest of the family.

Sophie cried while telling me her story. She told me how she felt anxious all the time and that she did not have anyone to talk to. She had a few friends at school, but could not confide in them because they may not understand what she was going through.

I did understand what Sophie was going through, how she was feeling responsible for her brothers, and how she was always afraid that something was going to happen to them. She constantly worried that she may not be there to protect them from dying like her first brother. It is a great burden to carry for a sixteen-year-old whose life is meant to be joyful and worry-free. She was supposed to be out playing and enjoying life. Someone else should have been taking that responsibility from her, but who?

I reassured Sophie and told her that God is responsible for His creation and He will take care of her brothers and that she had to take care of herself, relax, and surrender to a higher power. I told her that by taking good care of herself she could take better care of others.

Sophie left with a smile on her face. I hoped that her symptoms would resolve themselves and that she would trust life again where a whole new world would be waiting for her.

CHAPTER 16

GRIEF: DEATH AND DYING

'I am standing on the seashore. A ship spreads her white sails to the morning breeze and starts for the ocean. I stand watching her until she fades on the horizon, and someone at my side says, she is gone. Gone where? The loss of sight is in me, not in her.

Just at the moment when someone says, she is gone, there are others who are watching her coming. Other voices take up the glad shout, here she comes! And that is dying.'

-Henry Van Dyke

Another dimension of burnout is grief. How we do or don't grieve will affect our psyche and our ability to heal. We do not learn about grief in medical school or even about death and dying. It is something we need to learn on our own.

I remember when I was a young resident doing my rotation in obstetrics and gynecology, a family friend was admitted to the hospital for abnormal bleeding in her last month of pregnancy. The next day, I learned she had lost the baby. When we were visiting her during our rounds, we found she was devastated, bitterly crying, and very sad. At that time, I could not understand why she was crying so much. I thought, "She did not even know the baby, and she would probably have another one soon."

What a callous thought!

It took me years to understand loss and grief. It is not until I read the books *On Death and Dying* and *To Live Until We Say Goodbye* by Elizabeth Kubler Ross (M.D) that I understood the different stages of loss and grief.

I finally understood that although she did not see the baby, it was within her for nine months. She carried it, loved it, and anticipated the birth. The baby was part of her and it was enough for her to know and get attached to it. When she lost the baby, it was like losing a part of her. This was a great loss and she needed to grieve that loss before she could go on.

I do not remember grieving for my father when I lost him. I was five years old and I don't think I understood what death meant at the time. I have vague memories of my father holding the side of my face when I would get haircuts at the local barber in my hometown, Mehaidse. He used to put a plank of wood on the arms of the chair so I could sit on it to be high enough to have my haircut. My father used to stand next to me, support my head on one side while the barber was cutting the other side. A very tender moment in my memory – my head in the hands of my father.

One day in the winter of 1984, I was driving on highway 95 near Buffalo, New York on my way home from Roswell Park. It was the year I read *Death and Dying* and the same year I was doing a fellowship in Urologic Oncology and seeing people die of cancer, undergo surgery and extensive chemotherapy, and become very sick. It was the year I wanted to avoid contact with dying patients because I did not know how to deal with death. While driving on that highway on a cold, winter night, I remembered my father and suddenly burst into tears. I had to stop by the side of the road because my emotions were overwhelming. In his absence I told him how much I missed him and how much I loved him. I asked him why he had to leave me so early. That was the first time I grieved for the loss of my father. I was twenty-nine years old.

Loss and grief are part of life, but if we do not learn how to grieve and if we suppress our emotions, one day the gate will open and we will get flooded and be overwhelmed by it.

We also must make peace with our own death. Learn that life is impermanent, death is evident, and although we do not know the time or place, eventually it is going to happen. We need to be prepared to ask ourselves the great questions: How do I want to be remembered? What do I really want to do or be before I die? What would be the most important thought on my deathbed?

It is never too late to live the meaningful life we want to live. To do this we also need to be open to letting people go when they are ready to face their Maker. Our efforts would be futile if someone had lost the will to live.

Phil's story

I remember one patient, Phil, who had advanced prostate cancer which had invaded the bladder and blocked his kidneys. There was a risk of his dying from renal failure. I was a very enthusiastic young urologist, so I offered to him and his family the option of putting percutaneous nephrostomies (tubes in the kidneys) to relieve the obstruction.

After we did that, he felt better and his kidney function started to improve. He went home just to come back in a couple of weeks, with his wife who was very distressed. She told me that she could not deal with this and that she could not keep changing the dressing around the tubes which were leaking all the time and that she was afraid to touch them. She and her sons had decided to have the tubes removed. I explained to them that this may put his life at risk. Later, they consulted another urologist who removed the tubes. I was very shocked because I thought I was doing the patient a favor by prolonging his life.

I was not aware at the time that quality of life is much more important sometimes to some people than just prolonging life. The family made the right decision for him, and he died a few weeks later with his family around him and in a loving environment away from tubes and medical equipment.

It took me few years to grasp the importance of this lesson, especially after I joined the palliative care team--to understand the importance of social and family support. As scientists and physicians, we mainly focus on the physical level, leaving the other levels to psychologists, therapists, or the chaplain. We forget that medicine is an art. The art of healing sometimes does not depend on a procedure or medication, but simply to listen and to be compassionate.

CHAPTER 17

TO LOVE UNTIL WE SAY GOODBYE

"How shall you find the secret of death, unless you seek it in the heart of life? For life and death are one, even as the river and the sea are one... In the depth of your hopes and desires lies your silent knowledge of the beyond."

- Kahlil Gibran.

Nasira's story

Another patient I saw in Lebanon while I was there was Nasira, a forty-eight-year-old woman diagnosed with cancer in the cervix of her uterus. The first time I saw her she had an obstruction of her two ureters (the tubes coming from her kidneys to her bladder) because of the spread of the cancer. Nasira was very aware of her disease and very hopeful that she would be cured with the chemotherapy that her oncologist was giving her.

I knew at this stage that her disease was incurable, but I was afraid to shatter her hopes with this kind of news. We inserted tubes (stents) in her kidneys to bypass the obstruction, with her family's approval, but I could not but explain to one of her sons that she was very sick as it is not a custom in Lebanon to tell the truth bluntly to the patient and the family forbids it. But Nasira had a fighting spirit. She wanted to get out of the hospital every time she felt a little better and to go home and continue her responsibilities for her children. She looked at me every time I came to visit her and asked, "What do you think Doc, when will I get better?" I said, "Soon. Your kidneys are functioning better now, so let us wait and see."

I was sad not to be able to tell Nasira the truth about her disease, and that she should put her life in order and prepare to say goodbye. But she was not ready yet. She lived for three more months and came twice to have her stents changed during this short period of time. The last time she came, she had the disease spread all over her bladder and I had a very difficult time changing her stents. I knew if they became blocked again I could not change them.

Finally, I took my courage in both hands and explained the whole situation to the family, telling them that this was the beginning of the end. They all cried, especially her sons and her mother who was still alive and who was devastated by this news.

During this conversation I made an effort to stay present, hold their hands, and even hug them. I knew how difficult it was for them. At the same time I also had my own battle to fight; I was a surgeon and I was supposed to cure people and save lives. They did not teach us in medical school how to deal with death or how to announce death. We only know how to run away from death and be afraid of it.

This was the first time I stayed with a patient and their family, day after day, answering their questions, facing death with courage, and teaching them to say goodbye. I believe that I do not cure people or save their lives – God does—and that I am only here to be a channel for his healing power. I believed that he put words in my mouth every time I came to the floor to face Nasira and her family. Without feeling the urge to do something to cure her, I found myself caressing her head when I approached her bed. At the time, this was foreign territory for me and I was navigating it with care and apprehension.

I explained to the family that the most important thing at this point was to keep Nasira pain-free and that all she needed at the moment was their love. They cried every time I talked to them. I had tears in my eyes, too, and it was very healing for all of us.

At one point, I told them that she would be more comfortable at home, surrounded by her loved ones, and in her personal environment. She deteriorated very rapidly the last few days, was incontinent, and was sleeping most of the time, which lead us to decide to transfer her back into the hospital.

Nasira died two weeks after her last admission to the hospital. She was surrounded by love with all her family around her – her sons, daughter, sisters, mother, and brother-in-law.

They all understood why we did what we had done and they knew that we could not help her medically anymore. They understood that we could help with our humanness, our love, our openness, and our support. Her mother said later that she was very grateful for our courage to handle the situation as we did and that she admired that we could do this on a daily basis and without burnout. The only burnout we might have experienced would have been our struggle to save her and give her more medications, while all the while blaming ourselves for the fact that we had failed.

In the end, I am thankful for God--who is responsible for life and death, sickness and cure, and health and healing.

CHAPTER 18

SPIRITUALITY AND MEDICINE

"Patients can and should expect their physicians to respect their beliefs and be able to talk with them about spiritual concerns in a respectful and caring manner."

-Christina Puchalski, M.D.

Why do we want to include spirituality in Medicine?

Because it was never absent. Whether we want it or not, spirituality is part of living, part of health and disease, part of our daily activities, and part of who we are. We are mind, body, emotions--and spirit. Spirituality is what gives ultimate meaning and purpose in one's life. "Spirit" is the energy aroused from within the deepest core of an individual person. Without spirituality, the physician becomes an engineer and the patient a broken machine. Although, as a physician, I did not learn this metaphor in medical school, I believe that spirituality is present in every encounter with a patient or with each other as human beings. Now, more and more medical schools are including the subject of spirituality in their curriculum. A study published in the Archives of Internal Medicine in 2001 showed that spiritual struggles such as feeling abandoned by God increased the risk of dying by as much as 28% during a 2-year study done on elderly, hospitalized patients.

As I said before, Larry Dossey (M.D.) defines this new era in medicine as Era III. With Era I being Conventional Medicine, Era II being Mind-Body Medicine and Era III being Spirituality and the Human Consciousness in Medicine.

Christina Puchalski (M.D.) Director of Education, NIHR, suggested a spiritual questionnaire for patients, as part of the review of systems, where the physician could ask the following questions:

1. Do you consider yourself spiritual? Do you have a religious faith?
2. How might your religious beliefs influence decisions related to your health?
3. How does your religious or spiritual community support you?
4. How might I address your spiritual needs?

Bernie Siegel, in his book, *Peace, Love and Healing* said, "If the power of belief has enabled something to work for someone, I am not about to use the authority of my profession to destroy its benefits"

The Medical School Objectives Project (MSOP) stated, "Physicians must be compassionate and empathic in caring for patients… in all of their interactions with patients they must seek to understand the meaning of the patient's stories in the context of the patient's beliefs and cultural values."

Many studies have shown the importance of spirituality and prayer in our healthcare system. A survey of Family Physicians in the USA from 1996 to 1997 revealed that 90% believe that prayer, meditation, or other spiritual disciplines speed medical recovery. On the other hand, only 20% reported that the topic of spirituality and healing was ever taught during their training. 71% believe that they should join their patients in prayer if requested. 83% believe that relaxation and meditation techniques should be a standard part of formal medical training for physicians.

In his book, *The Healing Power of Faith*, Dr. Harold Koenig from Duke University presents groundbreaking scientific evidence of the positive influence of faith on patient recovery and well-being.

Dr. Koenig shows how strong belief, itself, may affect immune system responses, lower blood pressure, and extend survival. His study involved thousands of patients and confirms that saying prayers regularly can be as effective as taking medicine. With this kind of proof, we need to learn to trust divine guidance.

Randolph Byrd, a cardiologist at San Francisco General, conducted a randomized, prospective, double blind experiment to study the effects of Prayer on 393 patients (192 patients were prayed for and 201 patients were not), admitted to the Coronary Care Unit over a 10-month period. The results were striking and his study was published in the Southern Medical Journal. The patients who were prayed for differed from the others remarkably in several areas. They were five times less likely to require antibiotics, three times less likely to develop pulmonary edema (CHF), required less intubations, had fewer cardiopulmonary arrests, and had less pneumonia.

Gary Zukav, in his book *The Seat of the Soul*[21] says: "Prayer is moving into a personal relationship with Divine Intelligence... Prayer brings Grace and Grace calms you."

God is the healer
(A friend's story)

One evening, I received a call from a friend of mine. "It is an emergency," he said, "my neighbor has very advanced prostate cancer and we need to see you." I instructed him to come to me immediately, wondering what the emergency was about. He came with the son of the patient in question. The son was a young, professional man, very concerned about the health of his father. He was questioning all the treatment his father was receiving without any improvement. I gathered all the information I could get from him and could understand his concern.

His father had metastatic prostate cancer which had spread to his bones. He had failed hormonal therapy and was now receiving chemotherapy.

The son asked me, "How long do you think my father has to live?" I was stunned by the question and I explained to him that since his PSA (Prostate Specific Antigen – a marker for prostate cancer) was rising and he was not improving with chemotherapy, it meant he was not responding to the treatment.

He said, "I want him to be present for my wedding in three months." I told him he could have a small ceremony at home soon and let his father bless him. He said that his father was barely awake now and very tired and that he slept almost all the time. I realized at that point that his father was dying. These descriptions were the first signs of eminent death. He said that his father had some moments of lucidity but not for long.

It is very difficult to tell a Lebanese young man that his father is dying. He continued asking me, "Do you still think he may improve with more chemotherapy?" I had to call up all my training about how to be honest with him. It was a critical situation, but I found myself saying, "It is very important at this point that he knows that you love him and is reassured that he was a good father. Let him know he did everything he *was supposed to do, the best way he knew how. Let him know that you appreciate him and you will be OK in his absence."*

I stopped at this point, seeing tears coming out of his eyes. He was touched with what I said and understood that it was time to say goodbye to his father. He apologized for crying and I reassured him that it is only normal in these kinds of circumstances for humans to do so. He continued crying for few more minutes and then, relieved and grateful, thanked me and left. He had done everything he could do to honor his father and care for him the best way he knew how.

I closed the door and wiped a tear from my eyes and thanked God for putting the words in my mouth to be able to communicate with people, relieve their suffering, and continue my mission as a compassionate healer.

CHAPTER 19

MISSION/PURPOSE/MEANING

"I slept and dreamt that life was joy. I awoke and saw that life was service. I acted and behold, service was joy"

-Rabindranath Tagore

Research has shown that having purpose and meaning in life increases overall well-being and life satisfaction, improves mental and physical health, enhances resilience and self-esteem, and decreases chances of depression.

We need to encourage ourselves and people around us to find meaning in their lives. Sometimes people who are very sick, overwhelmed, tired, or suffering from drug abuse, feel empty, without purpose, and desperate for connection. Studies have shown that mindfulness training can enhance their healing, promote awareness of thoughts and feelings, help them engage in self-care, and reflect upon meaningful experiences in life.

How do I find meaning?

Finding Meaning + authentic power

Assaad Mounzer, MD, MA, ACC, FACS

By engaging in meaningful activities, being mindful of what we project, and being aware of our intentions because they create our reality. The following are some qualities to be nurtured in order to reach meaning and (authentic power.)

Qualities to nuture

Intention: If I wake up in the morning and do not have a plan for my day or an intention to live my life according to my values, then it is chaos. I will be dragged from one activity to the other without knowing how to choose what is important and meaningful to me. Having an intention focuses my energy to engage in activities which are in alignment with my values.

P115 **Values:** Choose the values that are really important to you and that you would like to nurture. Values are like seeds. They need to be watered with loving, acceptance, kindness and perseverance. We can learn to stop for a second when we get angry or are triggered by an event and in that split second make a decision to respond in a kind way instead of reacting with anger. In other words, we choose our response, instead of being dragged around by our thoughts and emotions.

Inner peace: "Anything that disturbs my peace is an issue which needs to be resolved." Like President of the University of Santa Monica, Dr. Ron Hulnick use to say, "We need to be aware of what is disturbing us, take responsibility for our emotions and accountability for our actions." Exploring why we react the way we do, clarifying the triggers, and reframing our beliefs could be a major step in producing inner peace and genuine happiness.

> *"Acquire the Spirit of Peace and a thousand lives around you will be saved."*
>
> -Saint Seraphim of Sarov

Self-care: Taking care of ourselves so we can take care of others is one of the ground rules to stay healthy and engaged. We need to make the right choices and pursue them with discipline and self-compassion. When Dean Ornish (a cardiologist who was the first to prove that heart disease could be reversed with lifestyle changes) was asked, "How do you get people to change?" He answered, "You do not get people to change, you provide the right environment and the facts and you allow people to make their own choices."

Gary Zukav[21] said: "Only through responsible choice can you choose continuously to cultivate and nourish the needs of your soul and to challenge and release the wants of your personality."

Forgiveness: The best way to have a clear heart is to forgive yourself for hurting others, to make amendments and to forgive those who hurt you. Our worst enemy is our ego, when we get attached to our own righteousness and refuse to accept others' points of view. Self-forgiveness is a great way to heal our wounds from the past, whether physical or emotional. We are sometimes our worst enemies as the result of judging ourselves harshly for not being perfect. We forget that we are humans, we commit mistakes and we need to forgive ourselves and move on. We need to use our wisdom and discerning awareness to learn from our mistakes.

Reverence: Reverence is the ability to honor the soul within each individual as a sacred energy. It is a spiritual perception that we are all Souls having a human experience.

I'm remembering one day I set an intention in the morning to use reverence. I went through that day with a great sense of peace, looking at each one as a divine human being and greeting them with kindness and compassion. What an amazing experience. It was so enriching for me that I felt energized, enthusiastic, and fulfilled when I came back home later that day.

◎ Service: Like compassion, hope, faith, gratitude and forgiveness, service is a spiritual quality. Especially if your motivation is not to get something in return. The best way to heal is to lose yourself in the service of others with joy and loving. Sometimes seeing the suffering of others can make us forget our own suffering and realize our kinship with human kind.

◎ Gratitude: Gratitude is a sense of deep appreciation for what we have and for the people in our lives. It is an affirmation of goodness. It involves a humble dependence on others or even a higher power. It affirms our sense of connectedness.

Scientific studies suggest that gratitude can improve your sleep, enhance your romantic relationships, protect you from illness and boost your happiness. Research showed that gratitude, like mindfulness, produces changes in certain areas of the brain--the medial prefrontal cortex. This area is associated with understanding others' perspectives, empathy, and feelings of relief. Gratitude allows us to celebrate the present. It also magnifies positive emotions, and blocks toxic negative emotions (like envy, resentment, hatred). It makes us stress-resistant and to have a higher sense of self-worth.

◎ Trust: Trust your inner wisdom, and listen to your Inner Counselor, or Authentic Self. It is there that reside all the answers you have been waiting for. Trust that you are here for a specific purpose and that this purpose will be revealed to you slowly. Remember, life is a journey, not a destination. Dr. Koenig from Duke University affirms that spiritual beliefs and practices, when used as a source of acceptance, love and caring, could supply strength, increase self-esteem, and provide meaning and hope.

Man's Search for Meaning

*"Everything can be taken from a man but one thing--
the last of the human freedoms – to choose one's
attitude in any given set of circumstances, to choose
one's own way."*

-Victor Frankl

As Frankl saw in the camps, those who found meaning even in the most horrendous circumstances, were far more resilient to suffering than those who did not.

One of my favorite books is *How To Find Your Mission In Life* by Richard Bolles[22], where I learned that the kind of work God usually calls me to do is the work that I most need to do and that the world most needs to have done.

Soon, I adopted my mission statement: "The place God calls me to is the place where my deep gladness and the world's deep hunger meet. My mission is to do what I can moment by moment, day by day, step by step, to bring more kindness, more loving and more gratitude to this world and make it a better place--following the Leading and Guidance of God's Spirit within me and around me".

Dr. David Hawkins, a psychiatrist and a philosopher, classified people according to their level of vibrations. In his research with thousands of people, he discovered that more than 85% of people are at a low level of vibration, below 200 he calculated. People at higher vibrations are the people who are compassionate, kind, loving, and of service to others.

He continued to say that people at a vibration level of 300 could counterbalance the negativity of thousands of people, and people at a level of 500--the sages and saints of this world--could single-handedly balance the negativity of more than 10 million people. What an amazing affirmation of the power of good that is keeping our world in balance despite all the violence, wars and negativity.

Reflection

How to write a mission statement:

Creating a vision for your life requires a willingness to explore and discover what is important to you and what gives you meaning. This means opening to your inner wisdom and guidance.

A mission statement is a philosophy of living. You can choose what important values guide your life and include them in your mission. It is something you have been doing all your life, although sometimes you're not aware of it.

You are a unique individual, and you are here for a purpose. You alone can fulfill that specific purpose. So do not sell yourself short. You are special and your mission statement will reflect those special qualities you have.

Start with the end in mind—that which is really important to you. Then choose from the set of values at the end of this book and pick the two or three that are most important and meaningful to you. It is like an affirmation, but more universal and spiritual. Affirmations are usually specific toward achieving one's goals and you could have many--one for each level: physical, mental, emotional and spiritual. A mission is more like an umbrella identifying the qualities you are using to live a meaningful life.

Ask yourself these two questions:

What are my next steps to honor the calling of my heart?

What do I care about, in my world and the world in general?

Examples of mission statements:

"*I am a compassionate healer. I am living my life with loving kindness and understanding and taking the next step in my spiritual journey.*"

"*I am a child of God and I am fulfilling my destiny as a guiding light for others to find their own journey and purpose.*"

"*I am a successful entrepreneur leading my company with honesty, optimism, and integrity and creating a healthy environment for myself and my employees.*"

"*My mission is to be actively involved with my family and my community with selfless service and deep commitment and to make this world a better place.*"

"*My mission is to be a teacher and to be known for inspiring my students to be more than they thought they could be.*"

- Oprah Winfrey

"*My mission is to have fun in my journey through life and learn from my mistakes.*"

-Sir Richard Branson

"*My mission is to use my gifts of intelligence, charisma, and serial optimism to cultivate self-worth and net-worth of women around the world.*"

-Amanda Steinberg (founder of dailyworth.com)

CHAPTER 20

FINAL WORDS

"Be who you are and say what you feel because those who mind don't matter and those who matter don't mind."

-Dr. Seuss

Life is too short. We never know when our time will come. Death is certain, although the time of death is uncertain. Bring always to mind what is important to you. Set your priorities and remind yourself that today is a gift, which is why it is called "The Present".

Contemplate what would be important to you at the time of death. Is it all the things you typically worry about throughout the day? What will really matter? What is meaningful to you?

Live your life with attention and intention and show loving kindness to yourself and others. Remember what Mother (Saint) Teresa said:

"People are often unreasonable and self-centered. Forgive them anyway.

If you are Kind, people may accuse you of ulterior motives. Be Kind anyway.

If you are Honest, people may cheat you. <u>Be Honest anyway.</u>

If you find Happiness, people may be jealous. <u>Be Happy anyway.</u>

The Good you do today may be forgotten tomorrow. <u>Do Good anyway.</u>

Give the world the best you have and it may be never enough. Give <u>your best anyway.</u>

For you see, in the end, <u>it is between you and God.</u> It never was between <u>you and them anyway.</u>"

Wayne Dyer, in his book *The Power Of Intention*, asked people to think about the last three words they would want to say before they die:

Mine would be, "Listen, Listen, Listen..."

Listen to the sound of loved ones saying goodbye. Listen to the angels singing while accompanying my soul. Listen to the sound of God receiving me in his bosom saying, "Welcome back home, my beloved."

Remember:

1. Care for yourself enough to make your own health a top priority.
2. Live mindfully in alignment with your values.
3. Demonstrate gratitude and have a positive outlook on life.
4. Exercise on a regular basis.
5. Take time to regularly rest, and connect with nature.
6. Adapt to change and suffering, build resilience.
7. Use acceptance and equanimity. Acceptance is the foundation for developing inner peace, stability, strength, and wisdom.
8. Invest in meaningful relationships
9. Forgive yourself and others, repetitively.
10. Have a purpose and higher meaning for your life.

Be of service!

Mindfulness of Breath Meditation

Chose a comfortable, private space. Sit with your back straight. Clear your mind, Focus on your breathing. If you are sleeping on the floor, keep your mind alert. [lying?]

On the Physical level:

- Relax your muscles and release the tension. Start at the top of your head, relaxing your forehead, then the muscles around the eyes, your jaw muscles, and progressively go down to your neck, back, arms and hands then the pelvis, thighs, legs and feet
- Slow down your breathing (diaphragmatic)
- Focus on the belly expanding with inhalation and then relaxing with exhalation
- Results: Metabolism decreases. Heart rate and blood pressure decrease

Mental level:

- Observing and letting go of thoughts
- No judgment
- No attachment
- Neutrality
- Gentleness
- Give yourself permission to release all concerns and anxieties about the past or the future.
- Results: Attention is turned inward to concentration on each breath
- Observing/witnessing the composing and passing of thoughts, feelings, and sensations.

If your mind wanders, it is no problem. Simply bring your focus back to each breath and develop an attitude of acceptance toward whatever happens in the process. Develop kindness and acceptance toward yourself.

Mindfulness Practice

"Wake at dawn with a winged heart and give thanks for another day of Loving"

-Kahlil Gibran

In the morning:

Gratitude: When you wake up, call to mind the people and things in your life that you are grateful for. <u>Keep a gratitude journal</u>. Use your Spiritual Tradition to surround yourself with a healing light.

Focusing on the Breath <u>Meditation</u>: Start with 10 min, increasing slowly to 24 minutes a day. This will build your attention and concentration.

Set an intention for the day: Decide how you want to show up today. Choose one of the meaningful values you want to bring forward.

During the day:

Stop, before reacting: If you have a challenging situation, <u>focus on your intention</u> then choose to respond in a positive constructive way.

Keep remembering and repeating your intention: May I be … (include your value or intention), May I be safe, May I be happy, May I be healthy, May I be filled with loving kindness.

Pause: Take few breaks during the day to <u>remember your intention.</u> Breathe. Fill your daily mindfulness sheet.

Take Action: Use discerning awareness and wisdom to choose your next step.

In the evening:

Reflect: Review your day. Focus just on awareness. No judgment.

What happened? Did you react or chose to respond to circumstances today? What kind of values did you bring forward?

Use your wisdom to learn from your mistakes. Be gentle with yourself.

Remember: "The circle of compassion is not complete until you are in it"

Daily Mindfulness Sheet

P98

Write your intentions for the day:

Decide how you want to show up today in the world:

First Check-in: How did I do so far; what emotions did I experience and how long did they last?

Second check-in: How am I doing with my intention?

Third Check-in: What unskillful event did I do today that I am not happy with?

Fourth Check-in: Did I use my intention to transform an unskillful event into a skillful one? If not, how could I do that next time?

<u>Self-Care List</u>

Write your mission statement:

Write your affirmations:

Actions to take on the Physical level:

Actions on the Mental level:

Actions on the Emotional level:

Actions on the Spiritual level:

<u>Physician's Bill of Rights</u>

o   We have the right to be happy.
o   We have the right to practice without stress.
o   We have the right to give our patients the time they need.
o   We have the right to express our feelings.
o   We have the right to have fun and socialize with each other.
o   We have the right to grieve.
o   We have the right to be imperfect.
o   We have the right to be human, commit mistakes and learn from our mistakes.
o   We have the right to rest and relax.
o   We have the right to care and be compassionate with ourselves and others.

(Copyright: Mindful MD Coaching)

Values list

Acceptance	Accomplishment	Accountability	Achievement
Acknowledgement	Activism	Adaptability	Adventure
Altruism	Ambition	Appreciation	Assertiveness
Attentiveness	Awareness		
Balance	Beauty	Belonging	Benevolence
Bravery			
Calmness	Care	Charity	Cheerfulness
Commitment	Compassion	Concentration	Competence
Confidence	Connection	Consciousness	Consistency
Contentment	Conviction	Cooperation	Courage
Creativity	Credibility	Courtesy	Curiosity
Decisiveness	Democracy	Dependability	Dignity
Devotion	Discipline	Discretion	Duty
Effectiveness	Empathy	Enthusiasm	Equality
Ethics	Enjoyment		
Fairness	Faith	Family	Fearlessness
Fidelity	Freedom	Friendliness	Fun
Generosity	Goodness	Grace	Growth
Gratitude			
Happiness	Hard work	Helpfulness	Holiness
Honesty	Hopefulness	Humility	Humor
Inclusiveness	Impartiality	Independence	Integrity
Intimacy	Intelligence	Introspection	Intuitiveness
Joy	Justice		
Kindness			
Leadership	Love	Loyalty	
Making-a- difference	Merit	Mindfulness	Motivation
Obedience	Open-mindedness	Optimism	Originality
Passion	Patience	Peacefulness	Power

115

Perseverance	Playfulness	Prudence	Punctuality
Quality-orientation			
Restraint	Rationality	Reasonableness	Relaxation
Reliability	Resilience	Resolve	Resourcefulness
Respect	Responsibility	Reverence	
Self-respect	Selflessness	Sensitivity	Serenity
Service	Sharing	Simplicity	Sincerity
Skillfulness	Spontaneity	Stability	Success
Teamwork	Temperance	Thoroughness	Tolerance
Thoughtfulness	Trustworthiness	Truth	
Uniqueness	Usefulness		
Virtue	Vitality		
Wisdom	Willingness	Wonder	Worthiness

BIBLIOGRAPHY

1. Caplan, R.P. Stress, *Anxiety and Depression in Hospital Consultants.* BMJ 309(6964):1261-1269. November, 1994.
2. Shanafelt, TD. "Burnout and satisfaction with work-life balance among US physicians relative to the general US population." *Arch Intern Med.* 2012; 172(18):1377-1385. Oct. 8, 2012.
3. Shanafelt, TD. "Changes in Burnout and Satisfaction With Work-Life Balance in Physicians and the General US Working Population Between 2011 and 2014." Mayo clinic proceedings, Dec. 2015, Vol. 90, Issue 12, pages 1600-1613.
4. Oreskovich MR, Kaups KL, Balch CM, et.al. "Prevalence of Alcohol Use Disorders Among American Surgeons." *Arch Surg.* 2012;147(2):168-174
5. Robertson, D (2012). *Build Your Resilience.* London: Hodder. ISBN 978-1444168716
6. Epstein, RM, Krasner, MS." Physician Resilience: What It Means, Why It Matters, and How To Promote It. Academic Medicine: Journal of the Association of American Medical Colleges 88(3):301-3 · March, 2013.
7. Amit Sood, M.D., *Handbook for Happiness.* Mayo Foundation for Medical Education and Research. 2015.
8. Siegel, B. Love *Medicine and Miracles.* Book by Harper & Row. N Y. 1986.

9. Simonton, C, Simonton, S. *Getting Well Again.* Book Published by J.P. Tarcher, Inc., Los Angeles. 1978.
10. LeShan, L. L. *You Can Fight For Your Life.* Book by M. Evans & Co, New York 1977.
11. Remen, R., *Kitchen Table Wisdom.* Book by Riverhead books, 1996.
12. Siegel, B. Peace, *Love and Healing.* Book by Harper and Row. 1989.
13. Larry Dossey, M.D., *Reinventing Medicine.* Harper Collins. 1999.
14. Bruna, J., *The Wisdom of a Meaningful Life, the Essence of Mindfulness.* Book by Central Recovery Press, 2016. Las Vegas, NV.
15. West, CP, Dyrbye, LN, Erwin, PJ, and Shanafelt, TD. "Interventions to Prevent and Reduce Physician Burnout: a systematic review and meta-analysis." Lancet. 2016 (published online, Sep. 28, 2016) View in article
16. Krasner, MS, Epstein, RM, Beckman, H. "Associations of an Educational Program in Mindful Communication With Burnout, Empathy, and Attitudes Among Primary Care Physicians." JAMA. 2009; 302 (12):1284-1293.
17. Davidson, R. J.; Kabat-Zinn, J.; D.; Santorelli, S.; Sheridan, J. F. (2003). "Alterations in Brain and Immune Function Produced by Mindfulness Meditation". Psychosomatic Medicine. 65 (4): 564–570.
18. Lazar, S, Kerr, C, Wasserman, R. "Meditation Experience is Associated with Increased Cortical Thickness." Neuroreport. 2005, Nov 28, 16 (17): 1893-1897.
19. Candace Pert, PhD. *Molecules of Emotion. Scribner, NY, NY.*
20. Elder Paisios. *Spiritual Awakening.* holy Monastery "Evangelist John the theologian, Thessaloniki, Greece.
21. Gary Zukav. *The Seat of the Soul.* Fireside edition. 1990
22. Richard Bolles. *How to find your Mission in Life.* Ten Speed Press. 1991.

Other resources:

a. Executive Leadership and Physician Well-being: "Nine Organizational Strategies to Promote Engagement and Reduce Burnout." Review Article. Tait D. Shanafelt, M.D., John H. Noseworthy, M.D., CEO. Mayo Clinic Proceedings, Volume 92, Issue 1, January 2017, Pages 129-146.

b. "Effects of Comprehensive Lifestyle Changes on Telomerase Activity and Telomere Length." Dean Ornish and all. Lancet Oncology 2013;14:1112-20

c. *Anatomy of an Illness.* By Norman Cousins. Norton Edition. September 1979

d. *Mastery.* By George Leonard. Penguin books. 1991

e. *Wherever You Go There You Are.* By Jon Kabat-Zinn. Hyperion. 1994.

f. *The Discomfort Zone.* By Marcia Reynolds, PhD, MCC.

g. *Neuroplasticity and Mindfulness Meditation* by Richard Widdett, Western Michigan University. 2014.

h. Siegel, D. (2010). *Mindsight.* New York: Random House Publishing Group.

i. *When Things Fall Apart.* By Pema Chodron. Shambhala publications. 1997.

j. *The Prophet.* By Kahlil Gibran. Published by Alfred Knopf. 1923.

ABOUT THE AUTHOR

Dr. Mounzer is a motivational speaker and a talented coach. He is a semi-retired Urologist, spending his free time teaching Mindfulness to help people build resilience, avoid burnout and deal better with stress.

He is a Certified MLP (Mindful Life Program) Mindfulness teacher, a Certified Professional Life Coach, and member of ICF (International Coach Federation). He holds a Master's degree in Spiritual Psychology with emphasis on Consciousness, Health and Healing from the University of Santa Monica, CA. He uses his compassion and caring to support his clients, so they can reach their potential, in their personal and professional development. He says about himself:

"I am a student of life. I am your partner in discovering new opportunities for personal and professional growth. I am an expert in compassionate listening and I walk with you the extra mile--to support you in clarifying your goals, taking effective actions and living a meaningful life in alignment with your values and purpose."

Dr. Mounzer is also a philanthropist, he is the founder of "The Mounzer Foundation for Service and Education", and he volunteers with Rotary International to spread peace, and make this world a better place.

www.mindfulmdcoaching.com
www.burnouttoengagement.com
www.mounzerfoundation.org.